Ghosts of the Isle of Wight III

Gay Baldwin

CONTENTS

(Contents continued over page)

GAY BALDWIN

The first ever collection of Island ghost stories *Ghosts of the Isle of Wight* published in 1977, has now sold almost 25,000 copies since the first edition sold-out in just three weeks.

Gay Baldwin's second book on the supernatural also topped the local best seller lists and this current collection of 75 haunting new tales is the third in this popular series.

Almost everyone enjoys a good ghost story and these eye-witness accounts of spooky happenings all over the Island should send a shiver down many a spine.

Although not a 'proper' Islander, Gay has lived on the Island since the age of four, and was educated at Whippingham Primary and Carisbrooke Grammar Schools. Her career as a local journalist has spanned more than twenty years, much of this time spent as a news reporter and feature writer with the IW County Press.

She lives at Cowes, with husband David, daughter Victoria, and a collection of Siamese cats.

Gay is currently researching another book and would like to hear of any strange experiences of ghosts and hauntings that you may have had. She can be contacted by telephone on (01983) 294651.

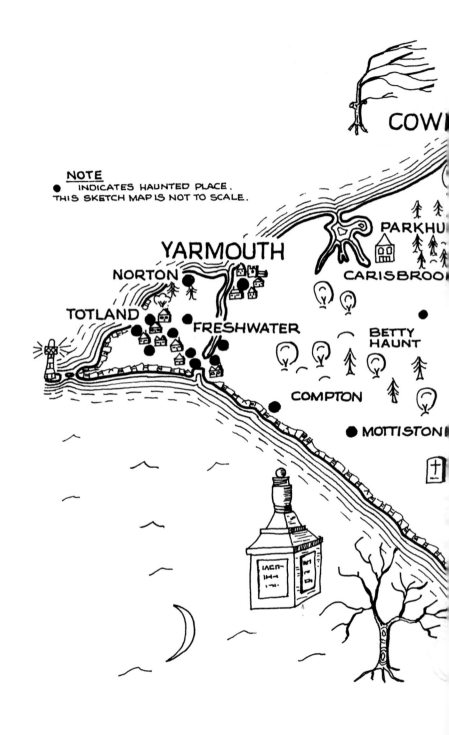

EAST COWES

WOOTTON

RYDE

HAVENSTREET

NEWPORT

BRADING

MERSTONE

ALVERSTONE

SANDOWN

GODSHILL

SHANKLIN

CHALE

BONCHURCH

VENTNOR

Map by Jack Street

Photo courtesy of the IW County Press

Parkhurst Prison, where an inmate serves a much longer sentence than the judge originally intended. (Chapter 6.)

"All Houses in which men have lived and died

Are Haunted houses: through the open doors

The harmless phantoms on their errands glide

With Feet that make no sound upon the floors"

Henry Wordsworth Longfellow

According to a recent survey, 44% of people in Britain believe in the existence of ghosts, and of these, one in seven claimed to have seen, heard, or been haunted by a ghost. The poll also showed that more than 50% of people believed in psychic phenomena.

Almost anyone can see a ghost. You certainly don't have to believe in them before they will appear. Some of the hundreds of Island people who have told me of their experiences are adamant that there is no such thing as a ghost. "I know they simply don't exist... but I have just met one!" exclaimed one very irate councillor.

Like their living, breathing, human counterparts, every ghost is different. Call them what you will, spirit, apparition, phantom or spectre, they do appear to exist in some dimension, although not necessarily our own.

Reports of supernatural happenings reach back to our earliest recorded history. Ghosts it would seem, have been around as long as we have. In more superstitious and devout ages, inexplicable happenings were recognized as works of the Devil. But in these more enlightened and permissive times people are adopting a more open-minded attitude. Many are becoming interested not only in ghosts and hauntings, but in other psychic phenomena such as near death and out-of-body experiences, extra-sensory perception, psychometry and the work of mediums and spiritual healers.

The number of hauntings and ghostly goings-on here on the Isle of Wight continues to amaze me. My two earlier books, *Ghosts of the Isle of Wight* which was co-written with Ray Anker, and *More Ghosts of the Isle of Wight* together look at almost 150 stories.

This third book contains completely new descriptions of ghostly happenings and experiences, with eye-witness accounts and exhaustive research. Some of the stories are amusing, others are puzzling, frightening or just downright bizarre.

Although I have endeavoured to discover possible reasons and explanations for each haunting — such as a sudden death or even murder — the cause of some supernatural happenings is totally inexplicable. Why should a ghost throw fruit and vegetables around every night, leave towels in a bath, or dabble in perfume on a dressing table. Their actions make absolutely no sense at all and I find them gloriously baffling.

With the help and patience of a great many people, I have put together a selection of stories from towns and villages across the Island, and I thank everyone for their generous assistance, particularly Mike Mackrill for some of the photographs.

Although I do not see ghosts, I do believe that certain other people can. I am in no way psychic or a sensitive myself, and I make no attempt to interpret or explain away these hauntings. Instead I talk to the witnesses, research any relevant history and write an account based on these facts. I leave it to you, the reader, to make up your own mind and draw your own conclusions.

In this collection of seventy-five new stories, you will visit haunted hospitals, meet some ghostly neighbours, encounter phantom undertakers, jilted brides and even enjoy a few spirits at the Island's many haunted pubs.

Meet Freda the ghost of Rookery Nook, the apparitions of soldiers, airmen, fishermen and grocers. There is even a blue-blooded Royal ghost. A few of the entities have violent tendencies but these are fortunately a tiny minority. One ghost is even safely locked away in one of the Island's top security jails.

All I ask is that you approach the whole subject with an open mind and if you ever meet a ghost face to face, don't be afraid. Try to remember as much detail as possible about the encounter... then tell me! ❦

Gay Baldwin

October, 1993

Chapter One
HAUNTING TALES OF NEWPORT

A GHOST'S JEALOUS LOVE

A young mother was so terrified by a jealous ghost's obsession with her baby that she turned to the Church for help in ridding her home of the undesirable spirit.

The vicar who cleansed and blessed the little terraced house at Hunnyhill, Newport, told Caroline Sutcliffe that her home was haunted by a rather pathetic unhappy ghost, probably that of a young woman who had lost her own baby and was attracted to Caroline's tiny five-week-old daughter Gemma.

"We moved into the house in the summer of 1984 and we loved it there... at first," said Caroline. "It was not until midnight on Christmas Eve that the haunting began. I woke up to find Gemma had been removed from her crib and was lying at the bottom of our bed on my feet.

"Neither her father Kevin, nor I had touched her, and I lay awake for hours worrying about it. The next day we were going to my mother's for Christmas dinner so I bundled Gemma up tightly in her shawl and blankets, wrapping a blanket around her moses basket as well, ready to take her with us. I left her fast asleep in the basket on the bed. But by the time I reached the bedroom door, about four steps away, she had started to scream. I turned to find her lying uncovered in the basket. Her blankets had been knotted together and were laid in a line along Kevin's side of the bed. Her foam mattress had been knotted in two places and thrown on top of the wardrobe.

"I just stood there open-mouthed. It had happened so quickly. It was impossible. I was in such a terrible state for the rest of the day that I rang my mother's vicar to ask his advice. He told me that I should move all the bedroom furniture around. It would confuse the spirit and put an end to the problem, he said."

Caroline carried out these instructions and for three weeks nothing further happened. Then fluffy toys and ornaments in the baby's room started to move about. "I would replace them and five minutes later they would have been

Hunnyhill, Newport — where a jealous ghost ran up an £800 electricity bill

swapped around again. It became a battle to have things in that room as I wanted them. It was always Gemma's belongings that were moved."

Then both Caroline and Kevin started to hear a woman's voice talking to Gemma in the night as she slept. It was a soft voice murmuring and crooning to the baby, comforting her. Once when Kevin was working downstairs he dropped his hammer. From the baby's room he clearly heard the voice say, "There there darling. Has daddy woken you up?"

A friend who came round one evening also heard the ghostly whispering coming from the baby's room. "She went upstairs to the bathroom and came down in a terrible state, white and shaking. She had heard a woman murmuring to Gemma and opened the door to see who was in there. Of course the room was empty except for the baby," said Caroline.

Night-time noises from the main bedroom became increasing loud and terrifying. There was banging and crashing which sounded to Caroline as if a heavy wardrobe had been repeatedly dropped from a great height onto the floor. Walls would rattle, and it was so bad that she apologised to her neighbours for the racket.

"They didn't know what I was talking about. They hadn't heard a thing — except for some beautiful music which they said drifted through the wall from the baby's room. They told me they stood on the landing to listen to it nearly every night. But I had heard nothing."

Things reached a climax one night when the noises started as Caroline was talking to her sister-in-law on the telephone. "She clearly heard them and couldn't believe it was the ghost. I rang the local vicar for help and he told me to keep a diary of what was happening.

"By this time I was so frightened that I used to carry Gemma around the house with me. I never left her alone. Every time I went up or down the stairs I went on my bottom because I was afraid of being pushed. I felt that whatever was haunting the house wanted the baby and not me," said Caroline.

Every morning she found that the net curtains in the kitchen had been pulled back as though someone had been standing at the window looking out into the garden. Each day they were pulled exactly the same distance apart.

Finally the vicar decided to take action and after obtaining permission from his bishop, performed a service of blessing in the bedroom and prayed for the unhappy spirit.

"He gave me a crucifix to put above Gemma's cot, which I still have, and from that day on, we had no more trouble," said a relieved Caroline. The vicar warned me that the baby would probably not sleep so well because the ghost had been there to soothe and look after her at night — and he was quite right — she did start to wake up more frequently.

"The vicar who could sense the presence himself thought that the ghost had probably suffered an unhappy violent marriage and had lost her own baby. He did not think she was menacing me at all, she just wanted to be near Gemma and was interested in her. But I am not so sure. I never felt alone there and I was very very frightened of what she might do."

By the early summer the ghost had gone, but Caroline and Kevin were still paying dearly for its sojourn with them. Although the young couple had only a very few electrical appliances in their tiny house, their electricity bill for the three months of the ghost's stay came to almost £800.

"We knew it was a mistake and refused to pay. Engineers who were sent to check the meter said there was no fault, but recommended that we should not pay the full bill because we clearly couldn't have used all that electricity."

However the powers-that-be insisted that the bill must be paid in full, and the couple struggled for months to pay the arrears. "I am positive that the ghost used that power in some way, but we could hardly tell Southern Electric that, could we? They would just have laughed if we had insisted it wasn't us but our ghost who had run up that bill."

THE HAUNTED GREENGROCERS

Every morning Joan Steel is the first person to arrive at a Newport greengrocers. And every morning after she has unlocked the shop, the first thing she does is pick up the fruit and vegetables which have been scattered all over the floor.

For the past twelve years, since Joan's daughter Maureen and son-in-law Rob Leal opened the popular Farmhouse Fayre shop in Nodehill, this has been her first task of the day... tidying up after a mischievous ghost or poltergeist.

"The oddest thing is that the fruit and vegetables are never bruised or damaged in any way. If they were, I would never put them back. But there is no mark on them. It's really quite bizarre."

Joan finds a mixture of fruit and veg all over the floor. It is a completely random selection of produce, and sometimes the place is a real mess. "It looks as if someone has had a really good time."

When she is alone in the shop, Joan won't go upstairs until other staff arrive. "There is an empty, cold feeling around the staircase, and on odd occasions footsteps have been heard on the stairs and from storerooms over-head. One young lad, Andrew who worked there for a time, refused to go upstairs at all at the end of the day."

Once Joan saw a black shadowy shape hovering near the stairs. It appeared to be the outline of a man which vanished into thin air.

Maureen occasionally notices the distinctive and very strong smell of a candle which has been snuffed out. This phenomenon always happens in the same front corner of the shop. "It's a peculiar odour but instantly recognisable," she said.

A ghost at this Newport greengrocers throws fruit and vegetables about in the night

"We have absolutely no idea why the shop should be haunted. It never bothers any of our customers and the ghost — or poltergeist — only seems to come out at night. There is absolutely no way that vibrations from passing traffic could be knocking the produce to the floor. It is simply inexplicable," said Maureen.

A former owner of the premises, Mrs Carol Armes of Newport, who ran 85 Upper St James' Street as a wool shop while living in the flat above, admitted she had often had an uncomfortable feeling that someone — or something — was watching her.

"We lived in a flat over the shop, and I would sometimes have a strong impression that there was someone else there. I never had any trouble with the stock though and fortunately I didn't have to pick it up off the floor in the morning."

Records show that in 1871 number 85 was owned by Mrs M Rugg, a wardrobe dealer, and the three-storey building almost certainly replaced an earlier dwelling, for Nodehill, officially renamed Upper St James' Street in 1861, is certainly a very ancient part of Newport.

Tradition has it that Nodehill is a corruption of Noddies Hill, named after the French invaders — or Noddies — who were buried there in 1377. The French were ambushed in Deadmans Lane (now Trafalgar Road) on their way to attack Carisbrooke Castle.

Perhaps it is the ghost of one of these long-dead Noddies which continues to wage single-handed war on the English using whatever weapons it can find... apples, oranges, tomatoes, cauliflowers and onions. C'est la guerre.

GENERATIONS OF GHOSTS

A three-storey terraced house in West Street, Newport, was home to two generations of ghosts. Mrs Gladys Ralph, who now lives in nearby Linden Road, remembers them well.

Built in the middle of the last century, the house became the Way family home in the early 1900s. Both her grandfather and great-grandfather died there and for years afterwards the family are convinced that their ghosts continued to treat it as their home. The sound of hobnailed boots would march down the corridor long after their owner, Edward Griffin Way, had passed on. Meanwhile, the ghost of Gladys's great-grandfather was seen by the family at various times in a first floor bedroom.

Although Gladys herself did not make his ghost's acquaintance until she was eighteen, she always felt nervous in the house at night. As a girl she had been given an attic bedroom which she hated. "I loved the air raids during the last war. I used to pray for them so that I would not have to sleep in that room," she confessed.

Because she was such an anxious child, tales of the family ghosts were kept from Gladys. So when she finally met the spirit of an elderly man with a white beard and piercing blue eyes, she was utterly terrified.

"I was staying at the house with my husband and our new baby. The babe was only a month old and I couldn't get to sleep. Suddenly a figure appeared to be standing at the foot of the bed. He moved towards me, floating round the old fashioned iron bedstead. He came between the cot and the bed and peered down at me. I just screamed.

Did the ghost of this soldier haunt a house in West Street?

"My sister and mother came running in and I told them what I had seen. They laughed and said 'Oh Gladys has seen the ghost'. I was told it was my great-grandfather who had died in that room many years before."

The family became quite used to the light-fingered antics of their ghosts. Jewellery would disappear completely — Gladys never found her cross and chain which vanished from the bedroom. On another occasion the decorative silver backing to a hairbrush was discovered twisted and melted in a fireplace.

Once, when the house was empty, Gladys and her sister Rhona heard those footsteps walking down the passageway and the sound of a brush sweeping the stairs. One night, the front door suddenly flew open and some unseen presence ran down the passage and up the stairs... into that first-floor bedroom as though it was late for a ghostly gathering.

THE HAUNTED SCOUT HQ

Did the ghost of a long-dead scout return to his old headquarters at Newport? Mrs Jean Gorzkowski is positive he did, for she saw him so clearly that even twenty years later, she can describe him in great detail.

"I was standing in the kitchen and saw someone pass by the window. When I looked again he was leaning against the door frame. He was between 20 and 25 with straight blonde hair. He had a very fresh, beautiful complexion and looked as though he was an outdoor type.

"He wore a pale blue shirt with pockets with flaps and buttons on either side. It was short-sleeved with an open 'V'neck and his arms were golden brown. I could only see his upper body. He was just standing there looking out into the garden. He was very real but I was not afraid. I was positive I was seeing a ghost," said Jean.

Ever since the family moved to the ground floor flat at Caversham in Whitepit Lane, strange things had been happening. The old house, built over a century earlier, had stables and orchards to the rear of its walled garden. In 1908 Caversham's owner Mr W. S. Pring allowed the newly-formed 1st Newport I.W.Troop (The Old Guard) to set up their headquarters in a small room at the back of the premises. The grateful scouts, who included a young Pring in their number, turned the derelict room into a cosy little club house, complete with a library, stove and gramophone.

Those pioneer scouts spent many happy hours there until 1913 when the Prings moved from Caversham. During the 1914-18 war a number of scouts from The Old Guard joined the Army to serve in France. Eleven did not return.

When Jean and her three youngest children moved to Caversham in 1971, she knew nothing of its history. However, she was soon aware of a 'presence' in the house, especially in the hallway and in her bedroom — formerly the sitting room. She often detected a pungent pipe-tobacco odour, although no-one in the building smoked. Her daughter June, would sometimes hear a man whistling, and Fiona, her younger daughter always felt nervous in the flat, especially after she woke at night to find her bedclothes being tucked in around her by an unseen presence.

In her kitchen, originally the conservatory, Jean found the cooker controls were being altered and turned up high. Door latches would move and the dog would bark furiously at something the family could not see.

"I am sure there were two ghosts in that house, the young man and someone much older and they may have had no connection at all," Jean said.

Matters came to a head when her youngest son, Martin, was rushed to hospital with an inflamed appendix. While the house was empty someone... or something deliberately broke a crystal sherry decanter and a fluted flower vase, then arranged the pieces under a table.

"I was very angry and I felt that things had gone too far and must be stopped. Perhaps I had subconsciously encouraged this presence. It had been

Caversham in Whitepit Lane was the original headquarters of the 1st Newport Scout Troop (The Old Guard)

almost comforting in an odd sort of way. Anyway, I spoke firmly to it and said 'This is quite enough. You are to go away and not come back. I am not going to have you damaging my house and things in it'."

From that day on, Jean and her children were troubled no more. Still very concerned about the hauntings, Jean called in her local vicar and asked him to perform an exorcism on the flat. But he refused, and told Jean he would like to wait and see what occurred next.

"I said I do not want anything else to happen, but he explained it may have been Martin leaving the house that caused the problem. He could have been the unwitting source of energy and when this was removed, the ghost, or poltergeist became naughty and broke things."

It was not until some years later when Jean discovered Caversham's scouting history that another piece of the puzzle fell into place. "In those early days of scouting they did not have the money to buy proper uniforms, they just wore shirts with pockets instead. Three of the young men were killed in action at Ypres. Did one of them return in spirit? We shall never know now."

The ghosts of a father and his young son were glimpsed here in Whitepit Lane

WHITEPIT WRAITHS

In Whitepit Lane itself, the ghosts of a father and his young son appeared to Island publican John Amies. The experience was so vivid that more than 40 years later he can still recall it with perfect clarity.

"I was just a lad and I was running along the road one day when a man and boy suddenly appeared in front of me. They were walking hand in hand.

"I was going so fast that I couldn't avoid them and ran straight into... and right through them. I felt nothing at all. I turned to look back and they had vanished."

John recalls that the pair were dressed in the style of the 1940s and the young boy had been wearing a school blazer, blue trousers and a school cap. "They had looked solid enough but as I ran through them there was nothing there." 🌿

Chapter Two
GHOSTLY UNDERTAKINGS

By tradition every churchyard is said to be haunted by only one ghost — The Watcher — who appears in a long white shroud or winding cloth. This ghost watches over the graves, guarding the dead and waiting for the moment to call on the next person in the parish who is due to die...

THE PHANTOM FUNERAL

A visit with family and friends to the picturesque Norman church of St Andrew at Chale turned into a bizarre lesson in living history for John Golding and his wife Mary. For as the couple, who live at Wellow, wandered through the churchyard with its grey weathered tombstones and ancient headstones, they noticed a small group of mourners standing at a newly-dug grave.

Funerals are a common sight in a country churchyard — however there was nothing ordinary about this one — the funeral those mourners were grieving over had happened at least two centuries earlier. The three figures standing with their heads bowed at the graveside were all dressed in clothing more appropriate to the 1700s.

Stranger still, as John entered the church itself, he felt time somehow slipping. Outside it had been a warm, bright summer's day, yet inside the 12th century church it was a dark and gloomy winter's afternoon.

"It was a very weird sensation. I was aware of the interior of the church changing as I stood there. Things seemed to move; the decorations on the walls altered; became brighter; and I noticed the figure of a priest in long white robes standing at the altar. It was as if I had somehow stepped back in time," said John.

"I didn't want to see any more and hurried outside again. The sun was still shining brightly, but the group at the graveside had vanished and I noticed that all the headstones in that part of the churchyard were old and weathered."

As John and his wife talked over the afternoon's strange experiences

with their teenage daughters and the friends who had gone with them into the church, he realised with a jolt that the others had not seen any changes to the church interior or noticed the strangely garbed funeral party at all!

Only he and Mary had glimpsed the re-enactment of that poignant little scene from long, long ago. Two centuries later, although both the deceased and the sombre mourners are reduced to bones and a handful of dust, their ghosts it seems, live on.

St Andrew's Church at Chale — the scene of a phantom funeral

THE GHOSTLY UNDERTAKER

At a quaint white cottage in Brading the apparition of an ancient undertaker, dressed all in black in an immaculate top hat and frock coat, mingles with the living at the house which was once his home. The elderly spirit is certainly not lonely at Rosebank Cottage, which is now owned by Mrs Betty Howell, for he has been joined there by several ghostly companions.

Betty who inherited the charming and picturesque old wooden cottage from her great-aunt when she was just twelve years old, isn't bothered by the ghosts — especially as three of them are members of her own family.

The wraith of Betty's great-great aunt, Jane Wheeler, has been seen walking across a bedroom into a cupboard which once led to an original wooden spiral staircase. The old lady's figure has also been observed outside the house where she appears to be scrubbing vigorously at the front door step.

Rosebank, Brading, where a ghostly undertaker lives on

A hairdressing client of Betty's who called at the cottage one day also clearly saw great-great aunt Jane's ghost. The apparition of a very tall gentleman in top hat and frock coat was also visible to her, as was the ghost of a little man who was persistently pushing his cap onto the back of his head.

"I recognised the description instantly," said Betty. "That was my father, Jack Fowler. He lived here for years and he was always pushing his cap back like that."

Mrs Clarke, an elderly visitor who spent a night on a makeshift bed in the sitting room at Rosebank many years ago, passed an interesting time talking with the two ghostly gentlemen who had come in to see her. A local medium also saw the two elderly men, dressed as undertakers.

One place in the cottage, the dining room, can feel cold and unwelcoming. It was in here that the bodies were laid out when Rosebank belonged to the local undertaker almost two centuries ago. The ghost of a long-dead Elizabethan soldier was also present in the room, said the medium. She returned that afternoon with a prayer typed on a piece of paper which Betty was instructed to

Does great-great aunt Jane (seated right) haunt her old home?

pin on the dining room wall. "From then on the atmosphere in the room improved and it felt warmer," said Betty.

Originally built as a fisherman's cottage, Rosebank is constructed of lath and plaster with wooden cladding, and has been in Betty's family for several generations. It was once attached to the Robin Hood pub next door which her grandmother used to run, until the old inn was pulled down to make way for a Conservative Club, itself now demolished.

Sometimes Betty can smell the pungent and very distinctive odour of tobacco smoke coming from the room in which Fred, her first husband, liked to sit with his books and opera records, while puffing away at his favourite pipe.

It is conceivable that one or more of the cottage ghosts are responsible for other odd happenings there. One appears fascinated by the radio in Betty's bedroom and has an annoying habit of switching it on at full volume, usually between 2am and 3am in the morning.

Keys, loose change and other small objects often go missing, sometimes for days at a time, only to reappear when Betty has given them up for lost. She is still searching for the key to her jewellery box, even though she has never taken it out of the lock. It vanished one day and she had to force open the box.

"This cottage has always fascinated me. Even as a very small girl I loved it and I am never frightened by any of the presences here. I have no idea why there should be so many gathered in one place. I suppose that they all lived here at one time and to them it is still their home," smiled Betty.

Sometimes in the middle of the night she is woken by a banging noise coming from the dining room... perhaps a ghostly echo from the past when coffin lids were nailed down in readiness for a burial in the village churchyard nearby.

A TIRED OLD GHOST

Just along the road from Rosebank, a tired old ghost is always ready for his bed at a former hotel in Brading. The elderly phantom wearing a long white nightshirt haunts a bedroom at Old Kiln, Yarbridge, the home of County Councillor, Mrs Peggy Jarman.

Peggy and her late husband, Bill, moved to the 14-bedroom Nutbourne Hotel, as it was then called, in 1976. The oldest part of the building — once said to be the home of four smuggler brothers — dates back to 1646. At one time it was even known as The Smugglers and during renovation works, Peggy and Bill discovered a tunnel set deep in the hillside and a large chamber which they suspected had been used for hiding contraband. Outside are the remains of old brick kilns where chalk excavated from the nearby downs was heated and turned into lime.

The first Peggy knew of the ghost was when she overheard two regular guests talking at breakfast. They were discussing their rooms and one lady said quite proudly, "I am in the ghost room."

Another guest who often brought school parties to the hotel asked Peggy, "Did you know you have got a ghost in room three?" The worried owners offered to move him to another room, but he said he was quite happy where he was, and told them he had seen the shade of a little elderly man in a white nightshirt float across the end of the bed. The ghost had apparently come through the wall by the entrance to the passageway and seemed quite a kindly old chap, said the guest.

Although Peggy has not met the ghost herself, she has often had to straighten the bed after he has used it. "I usually went in to inspect the rooms after the chambermaids had been round, and in room number three, I would often find a dip in the middle of the bed as though someone had been lying there. I was always having to straighten the counterpane in that room," she complained.

Her brother, Charlie Wines, who now lives in the old cottage has not encountered the old gentleman yet, but he has reported hearing odd noises there at night — hollow bumping sounds — rather like barrels or kegs of contraband being moved around... as if the ghostly smugglers are still up to their old tricks.

THE HAUNTED BATHROOM

The mischievous spirit that shared a cottage at nearby Alverstone with Barry, a local photographer, certainly had a sense of humour — and a fetish for towels; hand towels in particular, which would always end up in the bath.

"Almost every day I would go into the bathroom and the towel would be lying in the bath again. It really was quite creepy," Barry recalled. "One day I left the bathroom while the bathwater was running and when I came back, the towel was floating in the bath. There was absolutely no way it could have fallen in of its own accord."

At that time, Barry was living on his own at the cottage which was built in 1869 as part of Lord Alverstone's estate for a farm labourer and his family. The bathroom had been converted from the old dairy at a later date.

"There was a definite presence in that bathroom and visitors to the house often remarked on it. It was a very cold house and I always had to have a fire going, even in the middle of summer — but the bathroom would never get warm. It was not a very nice room..."

Barry's dog, a collie labrador cross, hated the place and would not set foot inside, so all the time Barry lived there the animal lodged with his parents in Sandown.

He now believes a poltergeist may have shared that cottage. It was certainly noisy enough, and liked to rattle pots and pans around on the stove. Barry's aunt, who had lived in a haunted house herself, recognised the same 'aura' of the supernatural in her nephew's home.

Finally, Barry decided he had had enough of the poltergeist's pranks and called in the local vicar to sort things out. It didn't do much good. After Brian had sold the house and moved out, the new owners began to find their own hand towels turning up in the bath!

THE GHOST OF ROOKERY NOOK

The minute Roy and Margaret Heaven stepped through the door of Rookery Nook, a little stone cottage in High Street, Godshill, they just knew they had to buy it. Almost twenty years later, they are still in love with the place, and feel that the house owns and possesses them. If they go away on holiday, they can't wait to get home, and always feel relieved to be back.

In their absence, they are always sure the place is being well looked after... by Freda, their resident ghost. The family has nicknamed the spirit of their cottage Freda, not knowing anything else about her, or why she pops in occasionally to check up on them. She usually only appears to women, although the men can sense her presence.

Originally from the Midlands, the Heavens moved to the Island because Margaret is an asthma sufferer and they thought the Island air would help her. After raising a family, Margaret works part-time at a restaurant in the village, while Roy is an undertaker. Their three children, who now have their own homes, all love coming back to Rookery Nook, and say they never want it to pass out of the family.

Rookery Nook in Godshill village is home to a ghost called Freda

On their first night in the cottage, as Margaret and Roy slept on the lounge floor they heard the sound of footsteps crossing the empty bedroom above them. "We would switch the upstairs lights off, and they would come back on again," said Margaret. Their neighbour in the adjoining cottage, Villa Nova, asked them, "Do you know you have got a ghost?" Her cottage it seems, was also frequented by Freda, who had a habit of opening cupboard doors to look inside and switching the lights on and off.

However Villa Nova's present owners, Mark and Lorraine Saunders, report that all is quiet there now. They are intrigued by stories they have heard of Freda, but when asked if she was still about, "Disappointingly, no", Mark admitted.

Freda who appears to Margaret and her daughter Juliet as a dusky grey figure in an old-fashioned dress, haunts the front bedroom overlooking the road where she materialises every few months, often when something special is happening — like the evening Juliet was in the bedroom having a fitting for her wedding dress.

"Juliet felt someone watching her, and turned round, thinking I had come upstairs. Instead, it was Freda, our Grey Lady, who was standing just behind. She floated there for a few seconds, and then moved off, straight into the wall," Margaret said.

Since the children have left home, Freda hasn't appeared so often, although Margaret and Roy always feel she is near. "We are never alone in the cottage. There is always a presence there. Although Roy and the boys have never actually seen anything, they have often felt they are being watched."

Sometimes Freda rather annoyingly moves or hides household objects like keys, which will turn up again weeks or even months later. Only once has anything been broken, and that happened when the house was locked and empty.

Roy came home to find that an ash tray which was on the dining room table, had been neatly broken in two and the pieces had been placed in the middle of the floor, directly underneath the electric light.

That dining room, curiously, is always very cold. When guests are coming even the combined forces of central heating, a roaring open fire, and an electric fire can never quite warm it up. Margaret always notices a drop in temperature when Freda makes her appearance, but she is unable to explain why her cheerful middle room, with its wooden beams and a lifetime collection of old horse brasses, always feels so cold.

A psychic neighbour who ran a nearby tea garden, left the cottage abruptly one day, refusing to set foot there again, claiming it was an evil place. "She said that there were spirits there which should be dead and buried. When she went into the dining room, she felt dizzy and her voice started to sound funny," Margaret said.

On another occasion, a Shanklin man tapped on the door to tell Margaret he had just seen a grey lady out in the road disappear through her cottage wall. "He was on his way home from the nearby pub, the Griffin, so I am not sure how reliable he was or whether it was just a case of one spirit too many," she recalled with a smile.

Research into the history of the cottages, Rookery Nook and Villa Nova, shows they were built in 1834 by the Earl of Yarborough, and the Heaven's cottage was given to Mary Kemp for the annual rent of one shilling and sixpence a year for her and her two children to live in during her lifetime.

The semi-detached cottages were built on the foundations of an earlier dwelling which burned down and it is clear that the site has been occupied for many hundreds of years. Although Margaret has been unable to dig any deeper into the cottages' past she understands plague victims from the Black Death, which swept the Island in the 14th century, may well have been buried in pits nearby. The plague which was said to have been carried in the village water supply from Newchurch, devastated Godshill, sparing just thirteen inhabitants.

"Until we moved there, it seems that nobody stayed at the cottage for long. It is well known in the village that queer things happen here, but it is an extremely happy place for us. We love it," said Margaret.

Another curious thread running through the cottage's history is the number of women named Margaret who have made it their home. At least four of her namesakes have occupied Rookery Nook and even her daughter Juliet's middle name is Margaret.

One of Rookery Nook's former residents is the founder and owner of the Island's doll and toy hospital, at Brading, Mrs Margaret Munday-Whittaker. Now approaching her seventies, this Margaret lived at the cottage for two years until January 1953 with her husband and two young children.

"I was never very happy there. It was not a very warm or welcoming house," she recalled. "One room was always particularly cold, and despite a roaring open fire, we could never really warm it up," said Margaret, referring to the middle dining room.

She too had problems with the lights, although in the early 1950s they were still gas lamps — Godshill being one of the last villages in the Island to hold out against new-fangled electric lighting!

"I was constantly finding lights turned on, even though I am certain I had put them out before going to bed. We would come down in the mornings and find the landing light and the one in the dining room burning. My husband was always telling me off for wasting gas. But I know none of us had lit them. I was always nervous of leaving even the pilot lights glowing, and turned those off each night, but next morning, they would be burning brightly again. I worried myself into quite a state about it. I was very glad to leave the place." 🐛

Chapter Three

PUBS WITH SPIRITS

THE WHISTLING GHOST

A ghost at Newport's oldest pub, the Castle Inn, is often up and about in the early hours of the morning. Landlords there always know who it is because they hear him whistling.

"It's a peculiar tuneless sort of whistle and you generally hear it between 2am and 3am when the place is very quiet," said Mrs Elizabeth Taylor, who, with her husband Steve, ran the famous 17th century coaching inn, once a centre for cockfighting, until 1991.

The eerie whistling emanates from the old stables and Elizabeth heard it on a number of occasions, always at the same time, in the dead of night.

The whistler is said to be a phantom ostler — a stable lad or groom who hanged himself in the old hay-loft in the 1600s. A visiting psychic told the Taylors that the stable had a very bad feeling, but Elizabeth never noticed any atmosphere of menace in the pub.

Late one night when she was alone in the empty bar and the doors were locked for the night, she saw a white shape enter through the front door and move slowly across the bar. Oscar, the family's ginger tomcat, saw something too, as did their dogs. Whenever they went up or down stairs, the animals would always walk carefully around some invisible obstruction at the halfway point.

He may be more than 300 years old but the Castle's whistling ghost seems to have mastered 20th century technology and enjoys watching the pub's television and video. "It was quite irritating. We were always having trouble with the television in the bar. The channel would keep changing. Someone was using the remote control because you could see the control light flashing. We had it checked out endless times, but the set wasn't faulty," Steve recalled.

Next the Taylors started having problems with their video recorder. Channels would be switched while they were recording, but by then, they knew who was to blame!

The oldest pub in Newport, The Castle Inn, has a whistling ghost

After the Taylors left the Castle Inn to run the Newport Squash Club, Eddie Duff took over as licensee. He agrees there is definitely something which wanders around the empty pub at night. After he had been there six weeks, the old staircase door creaked open although it had been stapled shut. The bar was closed and Eddie was alone. It was just after midnight. Suddenly old horse brasses, which were nailed to a beam, started to move and the pub clock jumped off the wall and reattached itself to a nail lower down.

Eddie has also heard the whistling and agrees it always occurs between 2am and 3am. The first time it happened, he went down to check, thinking there was someone in the old stable yard. It was completely deserted.

And Eddie has also been having a spot of trouble with his television and video recently. "Perhaps I should think about getting Sky TV. It might be more appropriate for a ghost," he laughed.

The Red Lion at Freshwater, where a defrocked priest was arrested

CHILL AT THE INN

The Red Lion pub at Church Place, Freshwater, is another ancient coaching inn with a ghost. The late Ron Legg, landlord there for 35 years, and his staff would often hear a man's heavy footsteps trudging along a stone passageway and down the stairs to the back hall, although they never saw the owner of those treads.

Bryan and Anita Farrant, who took over the inn after Ron left, heard those footsteps too, but said that whatever was haunting the pub always turned up too late for a pint... arriving when they were closed for the afternoon.

At 5pm every day, winter and summer alike, their lounge upstairs suddenly grew extremely cold. "It was a very noticeable drop in temperature. The room felt icy for about half an hour — enough to make us both feel quite shivery — then it warmed up again. It was decidedly odd, but otherwise the Red Lion was a very happy pub with a friendly atmosphere where, apart from that half hour, the welcome was always warm."

All Saints Church, Freshwater, stands just yards from the village pub

Licensee Michael Mence, who took over the Red Lion in January 1993, is still waiting to hear those footsteps. He is quite prepared to believe that something does still walk in the old pub, parts of which date back to the 12th century and are contemporary with the original All Saint's church next door.

He has a theory that the ghost may be that of a disgraced clergyman, a Rector of Freshwater, Thomas Symonde, who was actually arrested one day in the Red Lion in the year 1394 and charged with smuggling wool into France. Much of the early smuggling in those days involved taking fine quality IW wool across the Channel to the continent. This long stapled wool fetched a much higher price in France than England and the trade was known as 'owling', no doubt because it was essentially a nocturnal activity.

The unfortunate priest was relieved of his comfortable living and defrocked, but the landlord of the Red Lion remained sympathetic and continued to supply the former cleric with his ale — not in the bar — but in a tiny cubby-hole upstairs, next to the main bedroom... at the end of that stone passageway.

Was he in the habit of drinking alone there of an afternoon, at about 5 o'clock perhaps?

A phantom fisherman haunts this old Shanklin pub

PHANTOM FISHERMAN

An ancient fisherman wearing oilskins and smoking a pipe continued to drop in for his tot of rum at an old pub in Shanklin although he had been dead and buried for many a year. The old man's earthbound spirit continued to haunt the lounge bar of the Plough and Barleycorn long after he had cast his last net. Former Coronation Street actress Joan Read, once landlady there, was convinced he had moved with her from her last pub, the Green Dragon, just down the road.

In 1975, Harry and Doreen Massey took over as licensees of the Plough and Barleycorn and moved with their five young children into the flat above the bars. "Everything was fine for a couple of days. Apart from a very chilly feeling at one end of the lounge bar, we liked the place," said Doreen.

Then they noticed their little dog, Brandy, behaving rather oddly. She refused to walk past one of the rear doors and one night Doreen found her baring her teeth and growling at an invisible presence. Doors to the toilets would mysteriously unlock themselves and the children were unaccountably nervous

The Plough and Barleycorn at the turn of the century

of going downstairs at night. That lounge bar always felt cold, and despite its redecoration in warm colours with a fitted carpet, customers seemed reluctant to use it, preferring instead to squash into the tiny snug.

One night after closing time, Doreen and several of the bar staff decided to confront whatever was haunting the pub. They set candles on the bar and sat in silence, waiting.

"Nothing happened, so after a while we blew out the candles and I went to bed, leaving all the glasses for the morning," said Doreen. "When I came downstairs the next day, however, I found every glass in the place was broken. They were all where we had left them but every one was snapped in half. It was incredible. I felt that the ghost was taking its revenge."

A few nights later she took her courage in both hands and decided to confront whoever was frightening her family. "I went into the lounge bar, closed the door behind me, and shut my eyes tight. Then I told it, 'Whoever or whatever you are, you are welcome to stay here as long as you do not bother me, or my staff or my family — or I will have to call someone in to get rid of you'."

Although her eyes were still squeezed shut, Doreen could sense some-one in the room with her. "There was just a whiff of smoke from a pipe and a tang of seaweed. Then it faded away and I knew I was alone again. Whether he had been standing in front of me or not, I will never know. I wasn't brave enough to look. I just walked slowly out and shut the door behind me. After that night, the pub never felt bad again."

Doreen told her brewery of the problems with the lounge bar, and they agreed that the room, a later addition to the old stone inn, had never been popular. Was the Plough and Barleycorn already haunted, or did something move in when Mrs Read brought furniture and other fittings from the old Green Dragon pub?

Now converted into flats, that building certainly unnerved a firm of mainland building contractors brought in to do the work. Doreen's husband, Harry, recalls that the workmen, who had a pint or two at the Plough and Barleycorn, couldn't wait to finish the job. They refused to work there after dark swearing they had seen tools moving about and that ghostly footprints had appeared on wet cement.

The next licensee of the Plough and Barleycorn, Mr Noel Browne, who moved in after the Masseys left, says all is quiet now. So perhaps the old fisherman took Doreen's words to heart and moved on... with his pipe and faint tang of the sea.

MURDER AT THE PARTLANDS

The Partlands Hotel at Ryde, recently voted the Grottiest Pub in Britain, continues to enjoy its well-deserved reputation as the Island's most haunted pub. Although she is never seen, the ghost of Victorian barmaid Lily Deacon still enjoys playing practical jokes on a succession of landlords and bar staff. Customers too, occasionally taste Lily's bubbly sense of humour.

Local rumour has it that Lily was murdered by a jealous husband or lover in the old stone cellars and her body bricked up in one of the old smugglers' tunnels down there. One licensee, Michael Harris, who spent three years at The Partlands, was convinced that Lily haunts her old bar still — and she is not alone.

The Partlands Hotel at Ryde — voted Britain's Grottiest Pub, it is also haunted

As well as Lily's young, rather naive and mischievous spirit, there is a malevolent black fury emanating from a man, possibly her jealous killer, who is unable to find peace.

When the Harris family moved to the Partlands they knew nothing of its haunted history but were quickly introduced to the resident ghosts. Mike, his wife Jill and children Joanne and Peter, would hear their names being called from an empty room and sometimes they would feel a malignant presence in the kitchen, cellars and passageway.

"Once the lights are out and the place is locked up for the night, you just want to get upstairs as quickly as possible. The feeling is so intense it makes your hair stand on end," said Mike.

Almost every night while they were living there, Mike and Jill would wake for no reason at exactly 3am. This experience was reported by another former landlady, Mrs Olive Bowden, who also noticed a strange earthy smell when she awoke.

The cellars at The Partlands, where the barmaid Lily Deacon was murdered

No-one has ever seen Lily but some customers have felt her, and once she interrupted a darts match by poking one of the players in the arm. The pub ghost seems to enjoy moving or hiding things such as keys, kitchen utensils and even a garlic press, but they are always returned.

"We never saw anything actually move, but were always finding taps on the gas cylinders turned off and pipes pulled out. That cellar was my pride and joy; nobody else was allowed down there but I would constantly find things had been tampered with," said Mike.

"It would run in cycles of roughly three months. Then, as if she got bored with that, Lily would move on to something else for another three months. Light bulbs were a constant problem. We were always replacing them, up to a dozen at a time, and sometimes they would last just four or five days."

Curiously, their dog didn't mind going into the cellars, although previous pub dogs have refused to venture down there. However, the Harris hound would not go near the Gents and disliked the kitchens. He would sometimes crouch there for no apparent reason, shivering violently with cold — or terror.

Paul and Diane Mattick, who took over the pub in 1992, knew the Partlands' reputation before they moved in, so they weren't surprised when the pub's gas taps started to give trouble, and their children refused to set foot in the cellars.

"I was a total disbeliever in ghosts, but I am positive that something haunts the pub and is tampering with the beer and gas taps in the cellars, especially on the real ale casks," said Paul.

Former barmaid Julie Lancaster knows the pub of old. As a girl she played in the cellars and remembers the tunnels. She, too, was used to the strange happenings at The Partlands and was familiar with Lily's little jokes. "Sometimes when you went down into the cellars you got the feeling you were being watched. I always said, ' Hello' to Lily when I went down there, and 'Cheerio' when I was leaving. It's only polite. After all, she does live there, doesn't she?"

DIAL 999

Whatever haunts the Solent Inn at Ryde made such a racket one night that landlord Chris Cooknell dialled 999 and called in the police!

"It was as if someone was throwing furniture about in the lounge bar beneath our bedroom. The noise went on for at least ten minutes but by the time the police arrived it had stopped. We really believed we had burglars, or someone downstairs bent on wrecking the place, and I was not about to confront them," Chris said.

However, when officers arrived to arrest the culprits, they found the bar was completely empty and not a stick of furniture was out of place.

"It was extremely embarrassing," admitted Chris. "I felt a right idiot. We had only been in the pub a few weeks when it happened. The police said 'You must have a ghost, mate' because they could find no reason for all the noise."

The next time it happened, a few weeks later, Chris and his wife Belinda went down to investigate for themselves. Once again, in spite of the thumping, knocking and scraping noises, nothing had been moved and all the doors and windows were secure.

Chris and Belinda have discovered the Solent Inn at Monkton Street has a history of ghostly incidents. Formerly the Strand Tavern, by 1871 it had become the Strand Hotel, when it was owned by Albert Kemp. Well known in the town, the Kemp family also owned the Royal Standard in Castle Street, the Esplanade Hotel and the local Turkish hot and cold bath house in Pier Street.

Barbara and David Inglis, Belinda's parents, were the previous landlords at the Solent and they recall some very strange happenings at the old coaching inn.

Impatient spirits unwilling to wait for opening time have been heard banging a glass on the bar three times to attract the barmaid's attention. Voices of ghostly customers were noticed coming from the empty lounge by a startled barman, who clearly heard one of the unseen drinkers say "Oh yes please."

Phantom footsteps move along an upstairs corridor at night and something pushes open the bedroom door. A local psychic recently told Chris and Belinda that there was a very active presence in the old pub, but assured

The police were called to deal with a noisy ghost at the Solent Inn

them it was not harmful. They have since learned that a former landlady committed suicide in one of the upstairs rooms, where her body was found hanging from a wooden beam in the ceiling.

"You can sense something is still in that room," said Chris with a shiver.

A GHOST HITS THE JACKPOT

A ghost at the Sloop Inn at Wootton Bridge seems to have hit the jackpot on one of the pub's fruit machines. Assistant manager Donna Peach heard coins being paid out in what sounded like a big win on two nights running last August... although at the time, the machine was switched off, the bar was locked and it was 2 o'clock in the morning.

A ghost at the Sloop Inn, Wootton, enjoys a flutter on the fruit machines

"It is a very distinctive sound and I heard it quite clearly. It was a very big pay out, but when I went downstairs to check, the place was empty and there were no coins to be seen," she said.

Other strange occurrences have been reported by staff at The Sloop. Former assistant manager Alan Stewart, actually spoke to the ghost one night, believing it was his sister Jan standing by the office door. When he walked through the bar however, he saw Jan cleaning tables on the other side of the room. "The figure was dressed in green and looked quite solid," said Alan. The locked door to the cellar has been found wide open, and something has also set off the pub's alarm system in the middle of the night, although checks showed there was no intruder... no human one anyway!

Whatever haunts the old coaching inn on Wootton Bridge seems fascinated by electrical systems, for as well as playing the fruit machines at dead of night, the ghost has turned its attentions to the illuminated pumps on the bar. When David, the manager, switched them on one morning, something turned them off again, one by one. He tried once more, but as the bar staff stood watching, the lights went out again in sequence.

"There is a definite presence here and I am sure it is a woman," said Donna. "She seems to haunt a particular area of the bar, office and cellar which was once a tiny cottage next to the original Sloop Inn. Some years ago the cottages were demolished and the pub was extended."

This theory was confirmed recently when a visitor came in asking to speak to Jan. The woman explained that she had been born in one of those cottages and that her Gran, a kindly old lady, had died there many years earlier. It was her spirit which was still around, she told Jan.

A phantom miller was seen at this old tide mill which once stood at Wootton Bridge

THE PHANTOM MILLER

When John Golding was a lad he spent his early years at The Sloop where his father was the landlord. "Our dog refused to go into an upstairs room over the public bar. He would go absolutely nuts if we tried to him put him in there," he recalled.

Local folk told stories about the old mill next to the Sloop, one of just six or seven tidal mills on the Island which were worked by penning the water at high tide. The mill dam was the causeway carrying the road across Wootton Creek and over a century ago there were daily boats from the old Mill Quay to Portsmouth. The mill ceased working in 1945 and was demolished in 1962. Part of the old machinery is now stored at Bembridge windmill.

In the years the old mill stood empty and derelict, voices and the sound of footsteps would be heard in the deserted building. Ghostly footprints appeared in the dust, and one night John saw the tall dark figure of a man standing on the quay outside the mill, which vanished as he watched. From his bedroom window which overlooked the quay he observed the same unearthly figure on two other occasions. Dressed in a mill worker's clothes from the 18th century the spectre stood motionless in the same place for a few seconds before disappearing. (See picture previous page)

POLTERGEIST AT THE BUGLE

A particularly pesky poltergeist once plagued the kitchens of the former Bugle Hotel in Newport. Licensee John Amies who ran the old coaching inn in the 1960s often saw objects being hurled out of the sink by unseen hands.

"Pots and pans would be thrown right across the kitchen. It was quite uncanny and more than a little frightening," admitted John.

The Bugle Hotel, which closed a few years ago, was used in 1648 by the Parliamentary Commissioners as their headquarters at the time of negotiations with King Charles I for the Treaty of Newport. In its early days it was the Bull Inn, but as bulls were also known as bugles, the hotel assumed this other name.

A pesky poltergeist plagued staff in the kitchens of the old Bugle Hotel, Newport —
Mothercare now occupy the Mew Langton off-licence to the left of the hotel doorway

By 1804 the Bugle was said to be "the best and chief hostelrie in Newport" and was the main departure point for coaches to all parts of the Island.

The mischievous spirit first made itself known when the hotel's old stable block was demolished and new kitchens built in their place. Local legend has it that in June 1621, Sir Richard Worsley of Appuldurcombe was mortally wounded after a sword fight in the street outside the Bugle Inn. He was carried to the stables at the Bugle where he died from his wounds.

"Whatever was haunting the place certainly had enough strength to throw those pots about," John recalled. Although he never saw whoever was responsible, members of his staff claimed to have seen a man's figure standing in the kitchens.

"The rest of the hotel and the bars and restaurants were perfectly fine but there was definitely a strange atmosphere in those kitchens," he admitted. ❦

A phantom soldier haunts the Carisbrooke home of Peter and Chris Ferguson

Chapter Four
NEVER APPEAR WITH CHILDREN & ANIMALS

Sometimes children and animals seem able to see and hear ghosts that are completely invisible to adults. Often a child's tale is dismissed as imagination, but perhaps we should not be so quick to disregard what they see. It is possible that young children and animals operate on a slightly different psychic wavelength to adults and can tune-in more clearly to that spirit world.

THE SCARLET TUNIC

Steeped in history, the village of Carisbrooke sits in the shadow of its castle which has played such a vital defensive role in the Island's past. For thousands of years, people have lived, worked and died there — so it is hardly surprising to find their ghosts still walk.

Regiments were frequently billeted in Carisbrooke, much to the annoyance of many villagers — for the Army was notoriously slow to pay their keep — and at one cottage in Carisbrooke High Street, an unwanted lodger in a scarlet tunic still lingers.

The soldier's ghost has been seen, and heard, at the home of Peter and Chris Ferguson, where his earthbound spirit seems content to spend his retirement just a stone's throw from the old castle.

Although the cottage has been their home for almost 50 years, they have never seen the soldier themselves; he has only ever manifested for their children. The ghost first appeared to their young daughter Linda, who screamed when the man in a red coat materialised in the corner of her tiny first floor bedroom.

Chris dismissed this as a child's nightmare, but exactly ten years later, Douglas her youngest son, then aged seven, called to his mother and pointed at that same corner where he said a tall soldier in a red coat was standing. And if ever he was ill or feverish, young Douglas would stare fixedly at that corner, pointing and talking to someone his parents could never see.

The soldier obviously enjoyed music, for when Stuart, the Fergusons' middle son, took up the guitar so did the ghost. In the dead of night when everyone was asleep, music would be heard coming from Stuart's room.

The first time it happened the noise woke Chris, who stormed upstairs demanding to know why he was playing his guitar at 2.30am. But Stuart was fast asleep, oblivious to it all. His father laughed and said it must have been mice running over the strings. "Nonsense", said Chris. "Whatever it was, it always happened at half-past-two. There was never any tune that I could make out, just a twanging of notes. After a while Stuart started to leave his guitar outside his bedroom in the hall, or on the landing. It made him uncomfortable," Chris said.

After the children had finally left home, she heard that music just once more. But during almost half-a-century in the cottage Chris has grown used to lights being switched on in the night and the way ornaments and other objects are moved about the rooms. "Little things in this house are always going missing, although they turn up almost immediately somewhere else. Our ghost seems to be especially interested in cameras which are constantly being moved. Peter is a camera fanatic and has a huge collection of cameras and equipment which are often interfered with by unseen hands."

The little three-storey terraced cottage with its worn stone step fronting the pavement, was built in the 18th century on the site of an earlier dwelling used as a barracks by some of Cromwell's soldiers during the Civil War. Prior to that, Royalist soldiers — who may have worn scarlet tunics — were billeted there.

Whichever side he fought on, Chris and Peter don't mind sharing their home with the ghost. "There is always a warm and friendly atmosphere here. The house seems to almost cling to people in a strange way," remarked Chris.

"Neither the old lady who owned it before us, nor the one before that, would ever go out. Now I hate going out too. It is almost as if the house takes you over."

THE SIAMESE CAT WHO SAW AUNT EDIE

Cato the cat knew his new home was haunted... by an old lady who was fond of cats in general... but couldn't stand Siamese. "Nasty unlucky things", she used to call them, so when her cat-loving niece, Janet Eldridge, moved into her old home in Bellmead Lane, Newport, after her death, Aunt Edie was not amused.

Cato the Siamese cat met a ghost at The Purrings

Neither was Cato, who, sensing he was not welcome in the cottage, refused to set foot indoors. Whenever Janet tried to carry the Siamese in, he became agitated and ran out again. If shut in, he would sit outside Aunt Edie's old room and yowl at the top of his voice.

"He was a very, very unhappy cat and I was at my wits' end with him," said Janet, who for years ran the IW Branch of the Cats' Protection League at Ryde. "All my other nine cats were fine — it was just Cato. He would hide in a huge bramble thicket in the garden and refuse to come out. I was actually on the point of trying to find a new home for him. He howled, cried, paced around, and just refused to eat. It was pathetic to see."

Suspecting that her aunt's spirit still lingered in the cottage, Janet turned for advice to a friend and animal medium, Mrs Margaret Foster of Cowes. Margaret agreed to 'talk' to Cato and try to sort things out. She carried the cat around the house in her arms, talking to him all the time, and when she took him into THAT room his gaze was riveted on something by the window.

Whatever Margaret said to Cato worked, for he now happily comes into the house and has settled down at last. However, he still refuses to go near Aunt Edie's old room.

The old lady died peacefully in her sleep in the tiny cottage and Janet has very fond memories of the aunt who was like a mother to her. However the property needed a lot of modernisation work and Janet sensed that Aunt Edie was unhappy to see her old home being knocked about and altered. "She was irritable and unsettled and I could feel this. I did not want her to leave. To me it is still her house and always will be," Janet said.

Once again Margaret was called in. The medium could see the figure of an elderly lady standing at the top of the stairs holding a candle. She told Janet that her aunt did not like the alterations or the noise, and that she kept bumping into things. Margaret patiently explained to the old lady's spirit why the work had to be done. Satisfied, Aunt Edie said she was looking forward to Christmas with Janet in the house — and started to sing Jingle Bells, which had been her favourite Christmas song.

"I didn't want my aunt to be upset so I was very pleased that Margaret managed to settle her down and put her mind at ease," Janet said. "There are no bad or unhappy vibrations here now. I still sense Edie's presence sometimes, especially if I am feeling low. And I smell her whenever she is around, for she was a great believer in mothballs..."

THE PARROT AND THE GHOST

Polly the parrot saw a ghost one night at her Northwood home and actually said "Hello" to it. But since Polly's owner, Paddy Jardine, moved into the little cottage, once a part of the Ward Estate, in Pallance Road — or Tinkers Lane as it was formerly known, she has become used to curious things happening around her.

Shortly after settling into the old gamekeeper's cottage which dates back to 1870, bizarre things started to happen to Paddy and her children, Penny, five, and Peter, seven. In their first week there, Paddy found a number of torn bingo tickets scattered on the stairs. "I have never played bingo, and where they came from is a complete mystery," she said.

Next, a NAAFI shopping list dated 1943, bearing the name Sergeant Ashton, turned up under a chair. Then the family heard slow, heavy footsteps going up the stairs. At other times there came the sound of boots trudging up the front path into the porch. But there was never anyone there.

One night Paddy woke to see a dark figure going out of the room. Thinking it was her husband going to the bathroom, she turned over... and screamed. He was lying there asleep beside her. "We searched the house, but of course we found nothing," she said.

Once when she was alone in the cottage, Paddy heard a child sobbing outside the back door. "It was awful, that little child was breaking its heart, but as soon as I went outside the sound just stopped."

Ghostly footsteps and smells are common at this former gamekeeper's cottage at Northwood

Paddy, a retired school-teacher, and Norman Thearle, who shares the cottage, often smell an old-fashioned, very aromatic pipe tobacco downstairs — although neither of them is a smoker. This odour, which Paddy admits is quite pleasant, is usually around late at night or in the early hours, and started only after Norman moved in. Recently it has been wafting around outside the back door — and is powerful enough to completely mask the scent of hyacinths growing nearby.

And now, when Paddy is working in the garden, the smell of smoke has started to follow her about. "I have started calling him Smokey Joe", she laughed.

Another ghostly odour pervading the cottage very early in the morning is that of frying bacon, but Paddy only smells this in the front bedroom when the window is closed.

One evening not long ago, she was convinced something was wandering around in the front sitting room while she was in bed. "We heard drawer handles being rattled, and then Polly the parrot said 'Hello'. She only speaks if there is someone in the room and then only if it is someone she knows," Paddy added.

Occasionally as Paddy is standing in her kitchen, she will catch a glimpse of something passing the window. It is a rather creepy feeling and she knows she is being watched. However, she loves her cottage. "When you walk in the door it is as if someone is putting their arms around you and I don't ever want to leave. We are great collectors of antiques and interesting old things. It looks as if we have acquired a ghost as well."

GHOST IN A NIGHTSHIRT

An old man wearing a long nightshirt would often appear to a little Ryde girl when her family was living in a cottage in Weeks Road, once occupied by workers at a nearby hotel.

Tara Harvey, now grown up, recalls, "It happened when I was about six or seven. As I was lying in bed, an old man would appear near my wardrobe opposite the bed. It was a child's wardrobe and was probably only about four feet high. The old man, who was a misty white colour, appeared to be counting money or dealing cards, I could never decide which because I couldn't see the top of the wardrobe from where I was. I was never scared. The old man never spoke. He didn't seem aware of me at all and I never really saw his face, but I could sense he was friendly and meant no harm."

Elsewhere in the cottage, their home for eleven years, postman and local JP Ray Harvey and his wife, Mandy, knew nothing of their daughter's elderly visitor. They did however notice other manifestations which took the form of smells wafting through one particular room. "We used to get a very sweet smell, like jasmine, which would suddenly fill the lounge. It never happened anywhere else and we were at a loss to account for it. There was nothing in the garden with such a strong perfume and it always came at night. We even had the floorboards up searching for the smell, but could never get to the bottom of it," said Ray.

THE GHOSTLY SISTER

A long-dead Newport woman was seen by a young neighbour when she popped back for tea with her living sister. Many years before Darren Axford was even born, the two elderly sisters had shared a house in Medina Avenue. They were a familiar sight around town. One of them, Kathleen, had a hump on her back, and Judy Axford whose family lived nearby, remembers the sisters well.

"Their house was always filthy. Cobwebs hung from the ceiling like Christmas decorations," she recalled. Years later in 1981, when Judy was staying with her parents, her six-year-old son Darren often popped next door to visit Miss Doris, the surviving sister.

"One day, Darren went to have tea with her. When he came back he said Miss Doris had got a lady in there with her and they were both having a drink and some pork pie. We were very surprised because Doris never had callers. We asked Darren what the visitor looked like, and he told us she was a short lady with white hair. She was wearing a shawl and she had a funny back.

"We said nothing to Darren about what he had seen, but there was no way he could have known what Miss Kathleen looked like — she had died many years earlier, when I was still a girl. He wasn't even aware that Doris had ever had a sister," said Judy.

"Both were very genteel, old-fashioned spinster ladies who really had no idea how to cook, wash, or do anything for themselves. Their mother had seen to all that, and when she died, they were completely lost. That was why their house was always in such a mess. It really was filthy with plaster coming off the walls, although they always looked neat and tidy when they went out."

Only weeks after Kathleen's visit, Miss Doris died of a stroke. Shortly before her death the old lady told Judy that she had seen her long-dead sister standing by her window. "I think she has come for me," she whispered.

COMRADE IN ARMS

Shortly after Christmas 1992, as the old year drew to a close, the shade of a long dead soldier returned to an old house in Union Street, Newport. At about 2am one morning, postman Daryl Ambrosini was lying awake in his top floor flat when he noticed a sudden drop in temperature. The bedroom became icy cold and a feeling of great unease enveloped him. His eyes were drawn towards the window. There, standing with his back to Daryl, was the figure of a man. Like the Ferguson's ghost, this one was also dressed in a red tunic. Daryl could also make out the rest of his uniform which consisted of white canvas straps, light coloured trousers and polished knee-length brown leather boots.

"He was just standing there as though looking out of the window in the direction of Carisbrooke Castle. I saw him quite clearly for a matter of seconds, then he vanished. He made no sound at all and I never saw his face, just the outline of his profile. I was not aware of any sort of hat or headgear.

"I wasn't at all frightened — just surprised. I know it wasn't a dream."

PILE OF PIPE ASH

A little pile of pipe ash would sometimes appear outside Julie Matthews' kitchen window after a ghost had enjoyed his pipeful of baccy during the night. He was certainly a friendly ghost, for he often popped in for a chat with her son Danny, then aged nine, as he was about to go to sleep.

The family moved to their little terraced cottage in Field Place, Newport, in 1980 and settled in after some renovation work, which included re-positioning the kitchen window. They first suspected their new home was haunted when objects started to fall off the window sill. Nothing would stay on there for long.

All three of the family's lively Jack Russell terriers started behaving strangely, and would stare fixedly at something invisible to human eyes, following it with their eyes as it moved.

Then Danny told his parents that he had made friends with a nice old man who came into his room at night to talk to him. "We just thought it was an imaginary friend he had invented... at first," said Julie, now a JP living at Ryde, where she and her husband Geoff, run a sub-post office.

The family would often hear footsteps overhead moving around in otherwise empty rooms, and one night Julie actually glimpsed the ghost as he walked past her bedroom door. "I was sitting up in bed reading, waiting for Geoff to come home from his night's fishing. I heard footsteps coming up the stairs and saw someone standing by the door. I called out 'You're home early.' But it wasn't Geoff at all, it was the ghost."

When Julie's sister Pat stayed at the cottage for several weeks, she too encountered the old man. Alone there one evening, Pat came out of the bathroom to find the dogs looking at something at the top of the stairs. Following their gaze, she saw a figure standing there. It was an elderly man who appeared quite solid and real. As she recoiled in shock, he vanished.

Although she was unable to find out who the ghost could have been, she did discover that the cottage had a reputation for being haunted, and that previous owners had moved out in quick succession. "But we never minded the ghost," laughed Julie. "It was a lovely friendly cottage and he was completely harmless — if a little untidy." 🍂

Chapter Five
HAUNTED COWES

On the evening of March 15, 1941, the German Luftwaffe scored a direct hit on the searchlight post at Battery Road, Cowes, killing three of the soldiers manning it and injuring two others. Twenty-eight houses nearby were damaged in the attack.

Hotelier George Iddles was completely unaware of this event when he took his dogs for a walk in Battery Road one summer night more than thirty years later. Mrs Paula Iddles said that her late husband, an ex-Colour Sergeant with the Royal Marines, never believed in ghosts until that night when one walked right past him.

"We had just got home from our hotel, the Holmwood Hotel near Egypt Point, and although it was nearly midnight, George said he would take our dogs for a short walk before bed.

"He hadn't been gone many minutes when both dogs arrived home without him, very agitated and with their hackles up. George followed shortly after and told me he had just seen a ghost.

"At first he thought it was a motor-cycle policeman coming towards him wearing a helmet and long mackintosh, but as the figure drew closer, George could see by the light of a nearby street lamp that it was in fact a man in soldier's uniform of a tin helmet and army great-coat.

"He came up to George then veered off towards a nearby garden and disappeared completely as he walked straight through a high hedge. There was no gateway there. The figure just vanished into thin air..."

For several nights after that, George deliberately went back to see if he would meet the ghost again.

"Although we lived right opposite the turning into Battery Road, he never encountered the strange apparition on any other midnight walks. Whether he was relieved or disappointed, I really can't say," smiled Paula.

A GROWING SENSE OF EVIL

By day, Adrian Hume's home felt quite ordinary. But by late afternoon the atmosphere in the terraced house in Cowes grew more and more disturbing. His wife Sarah, their lodgers and guests felt a growing sense of evil, and a presence in the house. It grew so oppressive that eventually neither Adrian nor Sarah would sleep there, preferring instead to drive to Ryde to spend the nights with her parents.

Whatever was haunting the 120-year-old house in Newport Road actually appeared to Sarah, who is now Adrian's ex-wife, one evening in 1988, when she saw a young curly-haired man aged about eighteen looking round the bedroom door at her.

She had just left the room and was standing on the landing when she suddenly had an overwhelming urge to look back. There he was, seemingly aware of Sarah and looking extremely frightened.

"He appeared to be composed of solid smoke and after a few seconds he just dissolved into the air, growing fainter and fainter until he faded away completely," she said.

The feeling of menace in the house was centred around the hall, staircase and landing, where there was often a sensation of coldness. In the nearby kitchen, Adrian was startled when his metal detector started to buzz one night giving a very strong reading, even though it was not switched on.

Things finally came to a head when the couple went on holiday for a few days. In their absence a lodger who was a keen spiritualist, called in members of her Church to rid the house of the disturbing presence.

"Whatever they did seemed to have worked. The atmosphere felt quite different and we had no more trouble... for a time."

But then it returned with a vengeance. In February 1993 the emanation was growing stronger by the day. Three times in a single evening Adrian caught a glimpse of a ghostly figure flitting past the bottom of the staircase.

"When I saw it I just went cold all over. I was drawn into the hall and there I saw a featureless misty shape standing in the kitchen door frame. Then it moved away and drifted up the stairs."

The figure was also seen on the top landing by the bathroom. Adrian's dog, Spot, would grow agitated and bark at something there. The spirit's return disturbed Adrian badly. A computer programmer working at home, he was aware of the atmosphere building during the afternoon. It became so bad that he didn't want to go up the stairs. It was all he could do to bring himself to set foot on one particular step half-way up.

In desperation he turned to the Church for help. A priest from a nearby church agreed to come and bless the house, duly carrying out a ritual cleansing, using salt, candles and Holy water.

"It took about an hour. He blessed the water and sprinkled it all over the place, praying for everyone, both living and dead, who had ever lived in the house, and on the site before the house was built, blessing them and laying souls to rest.

"The priest said he could feel something was 'wrong' with the house and that there was 'something' here. He also added that cleansing and blessing houses was quite a significant part of his work — especially in Cowes," said a surprised Adrian.

"Whatever he did has worked. The house feels completely different. It is not a place I am afraid to be alone in any more. I just hope it lasts."

GHOST ON CRUTCHES

Meanwhile, just over the road, when a young schoolteacher woke in the middle of the night, she was more than a little surprised to find a ghost leaning heavily on crutches watching her from across the room.

Pauline Borodenko was staying at the home of her parents, Jean and Ken Robson, a 100-year-old detached villa in Newport Road, Cowes, in 1983 when it happened. She recalls, "I woke in the middle of the night and sat up in bed, my heart racing. Standing facing me was a very tall man in his forties with a beard. He was leaning on crutches and he was looking at me."

The solid-looking figure which Pauline believes was that of a naval man or sailor seemed to be about to speak to her. "He walked to the side of the bed by the fireplace and just melted away into the fireplace. I was left feeling puzzled but rather excited. I just wish I knew what he wanted to say to me."

Although she has never seen him since, Pauline's little daughter Elena who knows nothing of the ghost, refuses to sleep in that bedroom because she doesn't like the fireplace. Jean Robson, who has lived in the house since 1976, confesses that she feels uncomfortable if that bedroom door is left open. "I always have to shut it at night because it is next to our room," said Jean.

As to the origins of the ghost, the Robsons have discovered that the house once belonged to a naval man who was captain of yacht belonging to the Empress Eugenie, wife of Napoleon III. Could it be his figure which lingers in his old home... limping slowly about with the aid of a pair of old-fashioned crutches?

A ghost leaning on crutches haunts this house in Newport Road

THE YACHTSMAN'S GHOST?

It has served as a church, a theatre, a coach depot, a fire station and a college. The old Empire building in St Mary's Road at Cowes, has seen more than its fair share of change. Built originally as a church, it was also a Dame or penny school until 1908 when Tommy Little took his moving picture show and theatre there from its marquee in Denmark Road.

Many Cowes residents enjoyed film shows at the Empire until it closed during the thirties and was turned into a coach depot. During the war it served as an auxiliary fire station and in 1945 the building became the IW Technical College.

Since 1967 it has been the home of Spencer Rigging, the internationally renowned marine rigging business, whose craftsmen have rigged some of the world's top class yachts. The little adjoining cottage has been the home of Mrs Nellie Lord for almost 60 years and she knows the Empire building well. Working there as an office cleaner, Nellie heard footsteps on the old wooden staircase at night when the place was empty. She sensed a presence too, but was never afraid of it.

The old Empire building in St Mary's Road, Cowes, where a yachtsman's spirit was seen

During the war, part of the building was used by Cowes Spiritualists after their own church was bombed, and Nellie believes that this may have somehow guided spirits there.

More recently, two women clerks working in the office refused to stay in the building by themselves when the men had left in the late afternoons. "They were terrified of the place," Nellie recalled.

One autumn evening she actually glimpsed a ghost there. "I was washing up some cups when a young man appeared and walked over to a pile of rigging in the loft. He seemed to be examining it closely. He had very fair hair and was wearing a jersey and trousers. He was clearly a yachtsman."

The figure did not appear solid and vanished into thin air as Nellie looked on in amazement. The next day when she asked who owned that rigging, she was told it had come from *Morning Cloud*, the yacht owned by former Prime Minister, Sir Edward Heath, which was badly damaged off the Sussex coast en route to Cowes, in September 1974. Tragically, his young godson and another crew member had been swept overboard and drowned...

Right: A phantom coachman (see below) stands in a corner of the dining room of this house in Coronation Road

THE PHANTOM COACHMAN

It is usually towards the end of the year when a phantom coachman puts in an appearance at the home of Mary and John Austin in Coronation Road, Cowes. A solid muscular figure at least six feet tall, he stands motionless for several minutes in an old doorway in the corner of their dining room.

The ghost is impeccably dressed in black knee-length leather riding boots with a brown turn-over at the top, tight riding breeches, a long beige waistcoat and stock; he is also wearing a heavy long dark cloak with a short cape at the top. His dark wavy hair is drawn back and fastened with a bow.

"He just stands rather resignedly in the corner and I am not sure whether he is aware I am there at all," said Mary. "I have spoken to him and told him the year we are living in and that we now have Queen Elizabeth II on the throne. I have also said that if he is not happy still being here, I will do my best to release him or set him free. So far I have had no response. He simply disappears very slowly from the head downwards after about five minutes."

Although John has not yet encountered the ghost, their son Michael met him in the hallway at 2am. Michael however felt a sense of menace from the silent figure and an intuitive knowledge that it would be capable of violence.

"Why he should be here we have no idea," said John. "Our house wasn't built until about 1909 and this ghost is dressed in clothing which dates him about two centuries earlier. Maps and records show there was nothing but fields where the house is now, so where he has come from is a mystery."

Equally mysterious is the regular appearance of a little ghost-dog which is sometimes seen in the dining room around December time. The white creature, which resembles a Pomeranian, will suddenly appear and run around playing under the table for a few minutes before slowly fading away again.

"You just feel a draught as he goes past you. He doesn't bark or make a sound, but Kia our whippet certainly sees him, and Michael's cat spat at him and backed away hissing," Mary said.

Whether the two hauntings are connected, Mary and John have no idea for the ghosts never appear together. Meanwhile they are waiting to see what returns this winter...

SPIRIT AT THE COPPER KETTLE

A ghost from the Island's Tudor times is a frequent visitor at the Copper Kettle Restaurant in Bath Road, just off Cowes Parade. He generally puts in an appearance in September, and for Jean Craig who took over the Copper Kettle in 1979, he is always a welcome sight.

"He comes through the wall leading from the stairs to the cellar and wanders about the room for a few minutes. He comes and goes, but I always know when he is around. I think he is aware of my presence for I speak to him as a friend."

Jean is so well acquainted with Tom, as she calls him, that she can describe his appearance and costume down to the smallest detail. A solid-

The Copper Kettle in Cowes is home to a friendly ghost called Tom

looking being, his most notable feature is a partially severed right hand which has been burned and sealed in what was the time-honoured way of dealing with such wounds.

Tom has sandy-coloured hair worn with a fringe in a long page-boy style bob and his face is clean-shaven. His costume is made of suede or leather, with a hip-length tunic and large puffed Tudor-style sleeves slashed in the fashion of the time, with a green insert. He wears a sword and has a wide leather belt fastened with a very big brass buckle, puffed pantaloons, hose and rather crudely-made flat leather shoes with pointed toes.

His complexion is rather ruddy, as befits an outdoor type, a man of the land or some kind of bodyguard, which Jean feels Tom might have been.

"He was not a gentleman or nobleman, but he was not a poor man or peasant either," she said.

Jean puts Tom's age at about 32. "He is a very pleasant sort of person, not aggressive or dangerous and he looks at me with a knowing sort of half-smile. I wish he would speak and tell me what he is doing in the restaurant. I am often aware of his presence when I am in the cellar. Every time I go down there I say 'Hello Tom' and I hope that one day he will answer."

A visiting medium was able to tell Jean that her ghost's name was Tom but no further details were forthcoming. Why he should be haunting the Copper Kettle remains a mystery.

The prestigious Royal Yacht Squadron was once Henry VIII's castle, The West Cowe

Originally built in the 18th century and known as the Marine Tap, it was frequented by coachmen, male servants of the gentry and other well-to-do visitors who stayed at the Marine Hotel. It was also a favourite place of the press-gangs which gathered a rich harvest there among the scoundrels of the busy port — the deserters and smugglers.

For many years earlier this century the bar stood locked and empty. Finally, brewers Mew Langton offered it as a shop, and the old Marine Tap became The Curiosity Shop — an antique hunters' paradise — before being transformed once more, this time into The Copper Kettle.

As for Tudor Tom, why does he haunt the old building and how did he come by his partially severed hand? Was he a fighting man stationed at the nearby West Cowe fortress built in 1539 by Henry VIII, now the home of the prestigious Royal Yacht Squadron?

Jean has now left the restaurant and the Copper Kettle has changed hands. As for Tom . . . perhaps the new proprietors will make his acquaintance and discover why he lingers there. ❦

Chapter Six

VIOLENCE WITH INTENT

The majority of ghosts are harmless and appear quite benign and friendly. Some spirits however are not nice to know. The sensation of a disembodied hand grasping her neck was a terrifying experience for one young woman, while another was terrorised by a ghost with appalling body odour. Here a few encounters with vicious spirits...

SPECTRE AT THE OLD MILL

A ghost which enjoyed grasping people by the throat, once haunted a derelict old water mill at Yarmouth, where it revealed itself to a young Freshwater woman one night some years ago. Maureen Sutton can still recall the awful clutch of a disembodied hand locked around her throat...the piercing cold, and the shock as her neck was squeezed in that vice-like grip.

Maureen had gone with her boyfriend at that time, a local fisherman, to collect the lobster pots he stored there. "I had never been inside before and I was curious to have a look around," she said.

"It was a dark, rather eerie place. It had been empty for years and the smell of river mud and rotting timber in the mill was almost tangible. I was going up the stairs when suddenly I felt a hand locked round my throat. It squeezed tighter and tighter. I managed to scream and my boyfriend came running as I rushed out in panic."

He had not seen or felt anything himself and thought Maureen had just imagined it. Some months later however, he changed his mind after hearing the strange tale a group of film students had to tell.

They were in Yarmouth to make a documentary film about the River Yar and had slept in the old mill. After just one night however, they felt uneasy. There was something malevolent in the place with them. One student just laughed. They were fools to believe in ghosts, he said.

Left: A ghostly rattling of chains was heard at old Yarmouth Mill

After a night spent alone there he changed his mind. He told of hearing the sound of chains dragging through the empty mill and of a hand at his throat which had tried to throttle him.

"When I heard this, I knew we had shared the same experience," said Maureen. "I have discovered that the old mill was once used as a temporary gaol for French prisoners of war. Did one die there in his chains and shackles? All I know is that whatever walked there by night was not friendly."

Built in 1793 during the Napoleonic war, the tide mill bankrupted its builder, William Porter. After its mill pond silted up earlier this century, the mill became derelict. It has since been bought by Londoner, Giles Taylor, to be used as a holiday home. The fine old building has taken on a new lease of life and according to Mr Taylor, whatever once haunted the mill, does so no more.

THE GHOST WITH B.O.

Budbridge near Merstone, is little more than a handful of cottages, a farm, a nursery, and an ancient manor house listed in the Domesday Book. Holidaymakers pass by without a second glance and few Islanders ever venture to the end of Budbridge Lane. It is, however, the scene of one of the strangest hauntings I have yet come across, involving a ghost which was exorcised from one cottage only to take up residence in a new home a few hundred yards away.

Doreen and Bob Arnold moved to Budbridge Gardens several years ago to run a smallholding with a few livestock. Their spacious cedarwood bungalow has five bedrooms and it was in the smallest of these that their daughter, Susan, first encountered the ghost with B.O.

He only appears in the winter, and the first time she saw him, a terrified Susan screamed so hard that her family thought she was being attacked. She was — but there was certainly nothing human about her assailant.

She vividly recalls that dreadful night it all started. "I was asleep when all of a sudden something grabbed me by the neck. My duvet was yanked off and I screamed at whatever it was to get off me. I could make out a hat, shiny shoe buckles and a clay pipe. But the rest of the figure was in darkness."

A ghost with BO made a nuisance of himself at this Budbridge bungalow

Also accompanying the ghost was the scent of pipe smoke and the stench of an unwashed body. And whenever he appears, time — in her room and in the rest of the house — stands still. All the clocks and watches stop, and even the electronic timer on the video recorder is sent haywire. Little things go missing; earrings, keys, small change and pens are never found again. By now, the family just accept it.

Since that first night in 1989, Susan has been visited by the ghost many times. She changed bedrooms in a vain effort to shake him off, hoping against hope that he was haunting the room and not her. But in her new bedroom on the other side of the house, the small semi-transparent figure still appears, glides about the room, sometimes sitting on the bed, before walking off behind the door or into a wall.

There is a sharp drop in temperature when he materialises and Susan is becoming increasingly perturbed by the ghost's attentions. "Some nights I talk to him in my sleep, but I can never remember what I have said next morning. I just wish he would go away and stop bothering me."

Susan's little Jack Russell terrier, Twinkle, who always used to sleep on her bed, now refuses even to go into her bedroom. Her dad has twice been woken by a voice telling him, "Come on, Bob, it's time to get up", when the house was empty. He too has smelt the pipe smoke and heard the ghost moving around at dead of night. "Whatever it is, it seems to like our Susan," he mused.

"Stranger still, it seems that our ghost probably came from a neighbouring cottage a few doors down. This place was also once haunted by a violent spirit seen only by women, whom it would touch, grab and pinch."

There are astonishing similarities between the two hauntings for in both cases the ghost's appearance was heralded by the pungent smell of smoke mingled with the odour of an unwashed body and soiled clothes — and it was attracted to women.

Bob has been told of an exorcism carried out in that cottage in 1987 by a former vicar of Brading who was called in after the ghost became increasingly violent. The cleansing of that cottage was a complete success. The dirty old ghost was driven out... but not very far.

If the same ghost is responsible for both hauntings, why is it drawn to Susan? As far as the Arnolds know, their modern bungalow has no connection with that other cottage down the road. They were not even aware of the exorcism until the ghost turned up in their home.

Susan now sleeps with her bedroom light on to discourage him. But as she lies there on a winter's night, praying he will not appear, she sometimes wonders... where was the ghost between 1987, when he was exorcised, and 1989 when Susan first met him? How did he spend those two missing years?

JEALOUS GHOST AT THE DUKE OF YORK

A young girl attracted the jealous attentions of an elderly ghost at a Cowes pub, the Duke of York. Tracy Griffith, now married with a child of her own, was just eight when she moved into a little attic bedroom at the top of the seventeenth century coaching inn.

The ghost of a little old man would call in on her at night to tuck her in and have a chat. When it first happened, Tracy was terrified, but she grew used to his attentions and would often call upon him if she was feeling low.

The Duke of York at Cowes, where a jealous ghost was seen

"Even if he didn't materialise, I would know when he was there. When he did appear he always wore a torn red shirt with rather dirty old trousers and boots. I believe he came to me because we shared a love of horses," Tracy said.

In life, the old ghost with a long grey beard once lived in nearby York Street and stabled his horse at the Duke of York. One day according to local legend, he found the beast dead and was so desolated that he hanged himself from a beam in one of the old barns, said licensee Barry Cass.

The apparition was clearly protective of young Tracy and if anyone else slept in her room, he would try to frighten them away. International powerboat racing drivers do not scare easily, but Ritchie Powells and Bob Beech, who came to Cowes to race their powerboat *American Eagle* in the Cowes-Torquay Classic, awoke to find him bending over their beds and were also kept awake by organ music playing in the attics, said Barry.

The room's next occupant, a senior Gas Board executive, also woke suddenly in the night to find the old man's ghost looming over him.

When Tracy moved to a larger bedroom, the old ghost went too and remained with her until she left the Duke of York at the age of sixteen. "I can still feel something there now when I go back. He was never nasty, although I was scared when it first happened," she admitted.

Her mum Pat, who left the pub in 1989, never liked working in the kitchens because she always had the feeling she was being watched. She had an aversion to Tracy's old attic room, too, and always walked quickly past it.

One day she put her dogs, a German Shepherd and two Jack Russells, into that room and shut the door. "They went absolutely mad and were clearly terrified of something in there," she said.

And Pat always had to watch out if she smacked Tracy or had an argument with her. "Something bad would usually happen to me. One day after we had had words, I was pushed so hard by unseen hands that I fell downstairs. I think the ghost was a bit over-protective of Tracy," Pat said.

There have been reports of two other spirits seen at the old pub. One is a man wearing a very tall hat, short jacket and riding breeches. He is said to have been seen by a previous landlord who kept the Duke of York for more than thirty years. The other is a rather frail elderly lady in a black dress with her hair in a bun, who wanders through those old attics. Do they ever meet in the dead of night? It would be nice to think that occasionally they do.

A LIFE SENTENCE

A ghost at one of the Island's prisons is serving more than a life sentence. Inmates at Parkhurst Prison are understandably wary of a certain cell in A-wing where an unseen presence is said to sit on the end of the bunk.

Originally opened in 1838 and extended five years later, the prison was designed to hold more than 600 boys, some of whom were sentenced to be transported to Australia. In 1864 Parkhurst briefly became a women's prison, but five years later the jail was opened to male adult offenders and in more than a century since then, some of the country's most violent and notorious criminals, murderers and terrorists, have served time at Parkhurst.

The haunted cell came to the attention of prison authorities in the 1970s when its Irish inmate asked the warder on duty for a confidential word. He wanted to move cells, he told the officer.

"I don't care where you put me. I just want to get away from this one. There is something in here with me and I can feel it sitting on the end of my bed at night," moaned the prisoner.

Sceptical staff thought at first this was a ruse to get a better cell, but the inmate insisted he would go anywhere they chose if only he could get away from his own haunted cell. "We were rather intrigued by this and when we looked back in the old records we found that no-one ever seemed to stay in that cell for long. It was almost always standing empty. There were rumours that a prisoner committed suicide in there many years ago. But why his spirit has not yet found freedom is a mystery. He must feel at home here," sighed a long-serving officer. "He is certainly serving a longer sentence that the judge ever intended." ❦

The mysterious Longstone at Mottistone is a place of great power

Chapter Seven
HAUNTING FRAGRANCES

The appearance of some ghosts is often preceded by a smell, pleasant or otherwise. The fragrance of perfume, flowers, incense, or even the appetising odours of fresh strawberries, bread baking, or sizzling bacon are perceived by some. Old fashioned, pungent pipe tobacco is a very common phenomenon. Other smells can be more noxious or unpleasant; rotting flesh and even the "smell of death" have been encountered in a very few instances.

THE LONGSTONE... PLACE OF POWER

A family outing to the Longstone at Mottistone, one hot summer afternoon in 1981 turned into a very unnerving experience for a young Newport mother, Judy Axford, and her son Darren, then aged seven. Darren also had a strange encounter with a ghost in Newport, and this story appears in Chapter 4.

Judy explained, "We went for a walk to the Longstone with a friend and his little boy. The children were having a lovely time running ahead through the trees where there was some shade. It was a very hot day, but when we got to the stones themselves it was suddenly freezing cold, and I could smell something extremely unpleasant — it was like decomposed or rotting flesh. I was so cold that my flesh came up in goosebumps.

"I just wanted to rush away as quickly as possible, the stench was overpowering and I turned to go. As I did so, Darren started making the sign of the Cross, although he did not know he was doing it or what it meant. I suppose it was an instinctive gesture to ward off evil."

The Longstone, said to be a place of power, has long been associated with the supernatural. The 13 ft. high standing stone is now on National Trust land behind the old Mottistone manor house, and although its origins are unknown, its history has been long and sometimes steeped in blood.

Now associated with witchcraft and the occult, the Longstone has been used by the Celts, Romans and Saxons. The Romans turned it into a sacrificial altar to the god Mithras, offering blood and live bulls in their worship.

The Saxons are thought to have used the standing stone and its smaller horizontal companion stone as *moteres stan*, the stone of the speakers or pleaders, indicating a meeting place where the judge spoke or a person pleaded his cause. The village of Mottistone takes its name from this mote stone.

Over recent years the Longstone has been linked with magic rituals. Animal remains and occult symbols have been found there and two white witches have visited the ancient site to perform a ceremony in an attempt to cleanse it of its evil aura.

THE NUN WHO LIKED CHANEL

A nun with a nose for Chanel perfume is one of the spirits haunting the former Rectory at Chale according to previous owner Mrs Val Frost. During the two years Val and her family lived there, she would often find the tops missing from bottles of perfume on her dressing table and the levels going down — dabbed perhaps onto a ghostly wrist.

Mrs Betty Bryan of Freshwater, who spent a night at the rectory, actually saw the nun's ghost coming down the stairs in a cloud of perfume and watched her walk round the room, then turn and silently glide back upstairs.

The smell of perfume was almost overpowering, and as the nun disappeared, Betty noticed the ghost of a little old lady staring after her fellow phantom in stern disapproval. Val, who now runs a guest house in Eastbourne, never saw any of the rectory's ghosts herself, but she often heard, smelled and on one terrifying occasion, felt them.

The family moved into the rectory in 1980 after it was sold off by the Church of England, and they converted it into a guest house. Val was aware of the rectory's reputation for being haunted but was sure the former Rector of Chale for 33 years, Constantine Sinclair, was right when he insisted it was rats, not ghosts making the mysterious noises.

During their time at the rectory, Val and her three children quickly became used to strange things happening around them. There were heavy footsteps in empty rooms overhead; noises in the kitchen where pots and pans would be scattered; the electric kettle would be switched on; and the nearby

A nun with a nose for Chanel perfume once haunted Chale Rectory

radio would start up — perhaps the nun enjoyed music as well as her other earthly pleasures.

"After a while, nobody really bothered about it. I used to feel a presence there almost all the time, but it was a friendly feeling as though whatever was there was keeping an eye on us. I often had the impression that someone — or something — had just walked past, although there was never anyone there."

The family also learned to take no notice when ghostly fingernails would tap and scratch at the toilet door — though this did sometimes prove rather embarrassing for unwary guests!

Few visitors noticed anything odd about the rectory, but an Army major and his wife who stayed there were adamant they had been woken by a baby crying, although there was no infant in the house. The family's dog always refused to go upstairs and when Val tried to carry him up one day the animal was clearly so terrified that all his hair stood on end.

Perhaps he knew something Val didn't ...like the secret of the Brown Room. For whatever lurked there was definitely not benign or friendly, and after her encounter with it, Val never dared to set foot in there again.

All the bedrooms at the rectory were furnished in different colours and one night Val awoke in what was known as the Brown Room, to find herself being pinned to the bed by invisible hands. "It was impossible to move or even shout for help. I could feel my shoulders being pushed down and there was a tremendous weight on top of me. I could hardly breathe. I was completely paralysed."

After what seemed like an eternity, Val broke free from whatever was holding her and made for the door... but it wasn't there. The door which should have been opposite her single bed had vanished, to be replaced by a blank wall. With the room in pitch darkness Val felt her way around in a panic, desperately trying to locate that door. She found it eventually — where it should have been all the time, and flinging it open, Val could see by the light from the hall that the Brown Room was empty. Whatever had been terrorising her in the dark had left. But from that day on, she never set foot in the room again.

Subsequent owners, Terry, and Susan Taylor, admitted they had heard something of the rectory's reputation when they moved in, but put it down to village gossip. "It is a warm, friendly house and we have certainly never seen anything here," they agreed.

However, both Susan and Terry have heard phantom footsteps on the stairs. On one occasion Susan was in the kitchen with a friend when they heard the front door open and someone run upstairs into a bedroom. Assuming it was one of the children home from school, Susan shouted a greeting and carried on chatting. So when the children actually arrived, ten minutes later, she was rather puzzled — especially as the front door was still locked and bolted.

As to the origins of the nun and any other spirits Val encountered there, Susan and Terry are intrigued. The rectory, an old red-brick house, was built earlier this century for two sisters and was originally named Rose Cottage.

It later became the home of the Rector of Chale, and was sold off by the Church in 1980. Terry feels sure the house was built over an older dwelling but Church records have been lost, and further research has proved fruitless.

Susan, incidentally, has never noticed her perfumes being tampered with. Perhaps she doesn't use Chanel.

Strange ghostly smells plagued a family at this Northwood Cottage

SOMETHING WAS WATCHING...

When Peter and Wendy Taylor bought an old stone cottage at Northwood, near Cowes, the feeling of peace and tranquillity was almost tangible. "I just fell in love with it, the place was so warm and welcoming," Wendy said.

However, two years later she was not feeling quite so happy. The Taylor's side of the cottage, built in 1760 for an old sea-dog, Captain Ellice, was plagued by smells, most of them unpleasant. In the dining room there was the odour of something dead and rotting. This disappeared after a few days to be replaced by a far more acceptable strong smell of strawberries — in January!

Then six months later there was a bad odour of drains in the hall and landing — although Peter did not notice anything. This unpleasant and very strong smell would come and go, and despite inspections by plumbers, its source could not be found.

Then the peaceful atmosphere in the cottage began to change. "This was quite a terrible feeling and it seemed to be concentrated in the oldest part of the house. I would be sitting watching television and suddenly all the hairs on my neck would stand on end," Wendy shivered.

Both her daughters, Suzanne and Lindsay, hated to be left there alone. Suzanne complained that something was watching her and she felt it was the spirit of a woman. Then she started to be violently sick in her room at night and would wake in the morning feeling agitated and upset.

"I decided we could not put up with this any longer. I realised how much it was affecting our lives. In a strange way I was quite shocked and upset that something had the audacity to haunt my house," Wendy said.

A practising Christian, Wendy turned to the Church for help and her local minister and three Church elders came round to pray in all the rooms. Her pastor explained that the smells and vomiting were a manifestation of psychic energy which had been afflicting the cottage. After their visit, the cottage felt quite different, and since then Wendy has had no trouble. It is a happy and tranquil place once more.

THE SMELL OF DEATH

Can a deathbed still harbour the spirit of its last occupant? When Dick and Pat Hall brought a bed, in which a relative had died, to their Cowes home it filled the room with what they described as "the smell of death".

Dick, who still lives in that house in St Mary's Road, has now retired from Siemens Plessey where he was a senior technical monitor, but this experience was beyond scientific or rational explanation. The bed had been lent to his wife Pat's parents, so that her father could be nursed downstairs. Shortly after he died on the bed, Dick and Pat took it back into their spare bedroom.

"From then on that room smelt of death," Dick said. "Whatever we did, we could not get rid of it. The smell just would not go and it became so bad that Pat refused even to go into the room."

"I knew it was my Dad and he would not hurt me, but it got so oppressive that I would not even open that door and I was even afraid to stay alone in the house," confessed Pat.

One night Dick went upstairs and told Pat he was going to try to put a stop to the manifestation. As he walked into that spare room the stench hit him again. It was vile. "I spoke into the air and said 'Listen Dad, you are dead, but you are still clinging on to the Earth. Go and rest and we will meet you again one day. Good-night Dad, now leave us'."

Dick's little talk certainly cleared the air, for the next morning the atmosphere in that room was as fresh as a daisy. The smell had gone for good.

WHIFF OF TOBACCO

It was the smell of pipe smoke that first drew a Cowes man's attention to the old sailor leaning against the fence near the sailing club at Gurnard. Ken, who later emigrated to California, was fishing down on the beach when he noticed the old man there looking out to sea.

Ken called out a greeting, but in reply the old salt just vanished into thin air, taking his old clay churchwarden's pipe with him but leaving behind that faint but distinctive whiff of tobacco.

WARNED BY A HAUNTING SMELL

Did a Ryde woman's dead father return to warn her of impending danger? Amanda believes he did, and that he still keeps a benevolent and paternal eye on his family from beyond the grave.

It was a couple of months after her dad died from a heart attack at the age of sixty-two, that Amanda and her mum smelt his distinctive Old Spice after-shave filling the car. The two women were driving to Freshwater along the Military Road when they heard a rattling sound coming from the front of the vehicle. The noise grew worse, and when they arrived at her sister's house, Amanda had a look to see what the problem was. There was nothing obviously wrong, but on the way home, the rattle became even louder and the smell of Old Spice grew stronger.

Back home in Ryde, Amanda inspected the car more closely. She removed the hub-cap from one of the front wheels and was horrified to find all the nuts were missing. There was nothing holding the wheel on except for the four bolt studs protruding through the wheel's centre.

"How that wheel had stayed on the car I shall never know, because I had been going quite fast. When I got in the car to take it to my garage just down the road, the smell had completely vanished. It never came back. But I know my father was there in the car with us, trying to warn us of the danger and keeping us safe."

Amanda's garage mechanics, who had been working on the car the previous day, were also shocked to hear that the wheel nuts had come off. They put it down to vandalism, assuring her that they had tightened them correctly.

Since that extraordinary day, Amanda has never smelled her father's after-shave again. However she is convinced he is still close at hand and keeping a watch over his family — for her two young nephews still see their granddad and when they are misbehaving or fighting, he will wag an admonishing finger at them. But usually they see him sitting in the corner of the dining room in his favourite red easy chair....the chair in which he died.

THE GHOST CARRIES ON COOKING

Soldiers with the IW Rifles always enjoyed tucking into a plate of bacon and eggs cooked by Sergeant McBain, their canteen sergeant. At meal times the delicious aroma of frying bacon and eggs would waft through the old Drill Hall in Denmark Road, Cowes, making the men's mouths water.

The drill hall closed years ago and in 1970 was converted into premises for Strainstall Engineering Services. The old canteen is now used as offices and the building has taken on a new lease of life. Sergeant McBain however continues to tantalise the taste buds of Strainstall staff with his fry-ups.

The long-dead sergeant doesn't seem to mind that his kitchen has disappeared, he just carries on cooking. The smell is strongest in the area of the old canteen and is only discernible at night, when the building is quiet.

The men of Princess Beatrice's Heavy Brigade, the IW Rifles, moved into their new drill hall in January 1913 after it was opened by their Commander-

A ghostly soldier haunts the former Drill Hall in Cowes

in-Chief, Princess Beatrice, who was also Governor of the Island. Sergeant McBain lived in a cottage behind the drill hall, now occupied by Strainstall's resident caretaker Ray Luckett. Ray who has worked there since the early 1970s, said the smell of cooking and the sound of footsteps were often heard by staff working late in an otherwise empty building. "We all just accept it. He never bothers anybody and seems to be a happy ghost," said Ray.

Receptionist Mrs Marie Sawle also heard the heavy tread of those army boots echoing down what is now a carpeted corridor on several occasions, but she was not frightened either. Strainstall's managing director, Ian Welsh, has worked in the building since it was opened in 1970 by the Governor of the Island, Earl Mountbatten of Burma. He has both smelled bacon frying and heard someone walking along that top corridor while working alone there some evenings.

"It is really weird. There is a definite feeling of a presence there, and when you are working late, those bacon and eggs really do smell good," said Ian. "I sometimes wish Sergeant McBain would put in an appearance with a plateful." ❦

Above: A Heinkel He111 similar to the one shot down over Freshwater in the early hours of May 8th 1941

Below: An identification card for the He111 — as used by RAF pilots and anti-aircraft gun crews

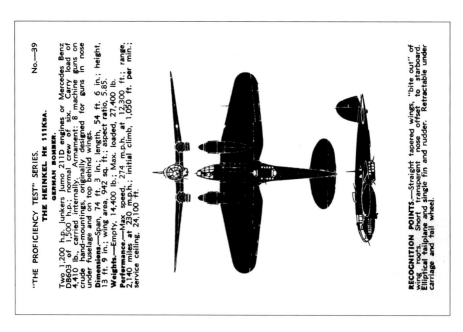

"THE PROFICIENCY TEST" SERIES.   No.—39

THE HEINKEL HE 111K5A.

GERMAN BOMBER.

Two 1,200 h.p. Junkers Jumo 211D engines or Mercedes Benz DB603 of 1,500 h.p.; normal crew of six. Carry load of 4,410 lb., carried internally. Armament: 8 machine guns on crude hand-mountings, originally designed for guns in nose under fuselage and on top behind wings.

Dimensions.—Span, 74 ft. 3 in.; length, 54 ft. 6 in.; height, 13 ft. 9 in.; wing area, 942 sq. ft.; aspect ratio, 5.85.

Weights.—Empty, 14,400 lb.; Max. loaded, 27,400 lb.

Performance.—Max. speed, 274 m.p.h. at 12,300 ft.; range, 2,140 miles at 230 m.p.h.; initial climb, 1,050 ft. per min.; service ceiling, 24,100 ft.

RECOGNITION POINTS.—Straight tapered wings, "bite out" of wing roots. Short transparent nose offset to starboard. Elliptical tailplane and single fin and rudder. Retractable under carriage and tail wheel.

Chapter Eight
SOME WEST WIGHT GHOSTS

THE AIRMAN'S GHOST

Half a century ago, the battle for the skies above the Island was at its climax. Between 1940 and 1944, more than two hundred men, women and children were killed in air raids. A further 21 Allied airmen and 27 German aircrew died when their aircraft crashed here.

Years later, the ghost of a corporal in the Luftwaffe, who died when his bomber was shot down over Freshwater, frightened the life out of a young mother when she saw his charred and blackened face staring at her.

Now a grandmother living in Ryde, Sheila Mason still recalls that early summer evening in 1961 with a shudder. The memory of that grinning face has never left her.

Sheila had set out from the fish and chip shop in Freshwater where she had a part-time job, just after midnight. It was a very still, moonless night; there wasn't a soul about. The houses in Queen's Road were in darkness as Sheila pushed her bicycle up the hill towards home.

When she was only a matter of yards from her house where her children were sleeping peacefully, she glimpsed a movement in bushes across the road, and in the light of a nearby street lamp, saw a young man's face peering at her. As she looked more closely, Sheila could make out burned and blackened features and noticed that he was wearing what appeared to be a leather flying helmet. The man's hands clutching the bushes were also burned and twisted while his mouth was distorted into a horrible grin.

Although the figure was moving through the bushes, it made no noise at all; there was no rustle of leaves; it was completely silent. "I looked away and then back — he was still there. It was that grin that finished me. It made my flesh creep, " said Sheila. "I threw my bike down and raced up the path to my house, but as I was desperately fumbling for the door handle, I felt a hand on my shoulder. I froze."

Sheila turned expecting to see the awful figure standing behind her — but there was no-one there. "I flew indoors and I was in such a state I couldn't get the words out to tell my husband Len what I had seen. Finally I managed to blurt out what had happened and he ran outside to look for the man.

"The road was completely empty. There was absolutely no sign that anyone had been in the bushes. Nothing had been disturbed or trampled. Len ran up and down Queens Road and then went to the police station to report the incident."

The following day Len, who was stationed with the Army at nearby Golden Hill Fort, told his mates there what had happened to Sheila. Several of the men remembered that a German plane had crashed near to the Mason's home during the war. "That was no mortal man, but a lost soul", the soldiers told Len.

Research has shown that in the early hours of Thursday May 8, 1941, a Heinkel He111 returning from a night attack on the Midlands was shot down by RAF night-fighters. It was seen to burst into flames and roared like a blazing fireball over the village of Freshwater before crashing into a wheat field about a quarter of a mile from Farringford House, the former home of Poet Laureate Alfred Lord Tennyson.

The petrol tanks burst as the plane hit the ground and two of the crew were blown to pieces. Two others had baled out. Oberfeldwebel Laube landed safely at the foot of the downs nearby and was quickly taken prisoner by soldiers who saw him descending in the beam of a searchlight.

The other man was not so fortunate. His parachute failed to open fully and he was killed instantly as he struck the ground, the great force of the impact leaving a deep impression of his head and shoulders in the ground. The dead aircrew were Unteroffizieren K. Dillinger, A. Habaereiter and W. Range.

Bus driver John Hall of Arnold Villas, Freshwater, who was a lad of nine at the time, still recalls that crash which lit up the sky all over Freshwater. Early next morning he and his friends went out hunting for souvenirs from the wreckage which was scattered over a wide area.

"There wasn't much left of the aircraft after the explosion. I'm glad that Oberfeldwebel Laube survived though because he was a regular visitor to the Island before the war, and he often used to stay at Gunville with a local family named Blow," recalled John. "It's very strange but even after all these years, nothing will ever grow on the place where the plane actually crashed."

Hill House, Freshwater, the scene of a duel to the death

Did Sheila see the charred and blackened ghost of one of these unfortunate men, exactly twenty years after their terrible deaths?

A small close of houses has been built on the site where the phantom airman appeared to her that night. Perhaps his spirit has now moved on. But for Sheila the experience of that awful encounter remains vivid. "I lay in bed night after night remembering that face. More than thirty years later I still see it in my dreams."

THE PHANTOM CARRIAGE

Old Freshwater folk tell tales of a ghostly carriage seen driving up to nearby Farringford House, once the home of Tennyson. As a lad, the late Ron Legg always laughed at their nonsense... until he confronted those ghost-horses himself one frosty moonlit night.

An ex-Royal Navy man who served aboard the ill-fated HMS *Hood* in the last war, Ron was for many years landlord of the Red Lion pub at Freshwater (which is featured in chapter three). It was in 1946, while cycling home from a dance at Brambles Holiday Camp, that he had his strange encounter.

As Ron made his way along Victoria Road, he heard the sound of horses' hooves galloping in the distance. A country boy, he got off his bicycle and stood in the middle of the road, barring the way with his bike to stop their flight. The sound came closer and closer. Ron strained my eyes but could see nothing.

As he stood his ground, the ghostly sound passed by him and went on up the road. As it did so, the tempo of the hoofbeats changed, as though the horses were moving from a metalled road onto a gravel surface, then the sound faded away.

"It was not a tale I ever told many people in case they thought I was barmy," admitted Ron. "I am not afraid of the dark. I'm an old poacher at heart and many a night I have been out alone. But I have never experienced anything like that before or since."

A DUEL TO THE DEATH

A duel to the death and a tragic suicide could be at the root of a mysterious haunting at Hill Farm, Freshwater, according to owners Lionel and Jill Osman.

Parts of their original thatched farmhouse date back to 1676 and there is evidence of an even earlier building on the site at Norton, where the Osmans now run a popular riding stables.

Ancient records and deeds show the Bret family were living at Heil (Hill) as long ago as 1588, but when Lionel, a local councillor, and Jill bought the old stone farmhouse in 1964, they knew nothing of its haunted history or of a local legend that one former owner, James Bret, had been killed fighting a duel in the courtyard and that his distraught bride-to-be drowned herself in the millpond at Yarmouth.

It is believed to be her tragic ghost, dressed in a gown of blue, which has been seen wandering through the oldest parts of the house when it was a holiday cottage. One girl who glimpsed the ghost was so upset by her experience that a

Farringford House, once the home of Poet Laureate Alfred Lord Tennyson

doctor had to be called out in the middle of the night to calm her down. A few years later another child sleeping in that room fell ill with bronchitis, but quickly recovered, much to everyone's surprise. The youngster said that a beautiful lady dressed in blue had visited her during the night and told her she would be better when she woke the next morning.

Other visitors, including a local vet, have sensed a presence at Hill Farm, and Jill and Lionel's daughter Jane, once saw the ghost appear through a lounge wall, glide across the room and vanish into another wall.

Now married with children of her own, the eight-year-old Jane was curled up in an armchair reading a book when she noticed something rather strange.

"Mummy, a lady in blue has just come through that wall," she told Jill. Her sceptical mother dismissed it as a child's overactive imagination... until renovation work a few years later revealed a hidden doorway in that very wall.

GHOST WITH A GHASTLY SMILE

A family-owned bakery does not seem a very likely place to find a ghost, but haunted it was, and to such an extent that the local vicar was called in to rid the house of its unwanted visitors.

When the family first moved there to run a butcher's shop in the adjoining building, there was no hint of the events that were to cast a shadow over their lives in such a dramatic and unpleasant way. Recounting the story, several years later, from the safety and comfort of her Parkhurst home, Mrs Beryl Green, who is now divorced, can scarcely believe what the family went through.

When her former husband, a qualified butcher, opened his own business, the family moved into a three-storey, turn-of-the-century house adjoining the shop, which they converted into a small bakery with flats above. Clare, then five, was the first to notice something untoward at the house. It was an event that haunts her to this day. She can still vividly picture the old man wearing a nightgown and cap who leered round her bedroom door before disappearing into the wall.

"He was not very tall, and he had protruding teeth, a thin face and a ghastly smile. I was reading my book and as I looked up, I saw him there, watching me," she said with a shiver. As the apparition came into the room, the door moved slightly, and he simply walked out again, through the wall. Clare's reaction to this was perfectly understandable, "I screamed and wet the bed", she confessed.

After that she would notice her large wooden rocking horse start to rock gently of its own accord, propelled by some ghostly hand. One morning in the bakery, freshly baked loaves jumped off the shelves where they were cooling, and both Clare and Beryl heard the sound of footsteps crossing empty rooms overhead.

Sometimes when she was playing her electronic organ, young Clare would feel a strange pressure on the back of her neck, which would make her physically sick. "That house was never a warm place. It always felt cold, even in the bakery with the ovens on. Our dog would just sit there and shiver," said Beryl.

The real problems however started after the family moved into a house just behind the bakery and let the flat to their son Gary and a friend. The eerie strains of violin music floated through the otherwise empty house when Gary and his girlfriend were alone there. Beryl heard music too when she called at the bakery with friends shortly afterwards. "We could all hear it, but as we walked upstairs, it stopped abruptly. After that we would hear a lot of banging coming from the kitchen on the first floor."

In an attempt to find the cause, Gary put a microphone in the kitchen and ran the wire down to a tape recorder and loudspeaker in the bakery. The sound of chattering voices could be heard, although no words were discernable. And nothing was ever recorded on the tape. "It was as if they knew what we were trying to do," said Beryl.

Matters came to a head at about 3am one morning when Gary and his father, who had been working in the bakery, woke Beryl in utter panic. They swore they would never set foot in the bakery again, even though they had left loaves baking in the hot ovens. They had heard the sound of people coming down the stairs and felt the building vibrate. All the dials on the ovens shot up to maximum temperature, and there was a terrible sensation of pressure as though something was actually passing through them, they told Beryl.

She telephoned two friends who were interested in Spiritualism and they came round immediately. All five went into the bakery, and Len, one of their friends, firmly ordered whatever was occupying the bakery to leave. "It was all very quiet. Then suddenly there was a violent banging from the very top floor. Up there it was freezing cold, an unnatural cold, and we found the light bulbs in the bedroom and hall were lying unbroken on the floor," Beryl whispered.

They went into the top bedroom together, and each felt a strange sensation of pressure, as if being pushed. Suddenly there was a tremendous booming sound and a rush of air towards them and out of the window. Then all was quiet.

Beryl later learned that the house had once been occupied by a very devout Catholic lady who had been a violin teacher and organist at her local church. This elderly spinster shared the house with her brother who liked to tipple — she used to regularly search the house for concealed whisky bottles. Other Spiritualist friends told Beryl that the old lady's spirit had not wanted to leave the house when she died, and strongly disapproved of Gary and his friend sharing the flat in what she still regarded as *her* house.

As the weeks went by, things did not improve and the family's nerves were constantly on edge. Paper used for wrapping the bread would rustle, the shop bell would ring although there were no customers. The bakery continued to be haunted. It was after a young couple who were renting the flat found their pillows spotted with blood, that the family decided to call upon their local vicar to bless the house and bakery to try to cleanse it of its troubled spirits.

"It did not work", said Beryl. "We put crucifixes in all the rooms, we always wear them ourselves — I never take mine off now. We did everything we could to move the old lady and her brother out. Finally we did the only sensible thing. We moved out ourselves!"

THE SPECTRAL HANDS

The sight of ghostly hands tearing paper off the walls of an empty house so terrified a little girl that even today, more than 30 years later, she feels uneasy driving past it. Now the wife of an Army officer, Mrs Maureen Sutton of Freshwater, still dreams of that house in nearby Summers Lane, Middleton.

She and a friend had gone to the home of her aunt, who had recently died, to fetch some books, but when the girls arrived, they realised they had forgotten the key. Rather than walk all the way home for it, they climbed in through an open bedroom window upstairs and tiptoed through the room. Crossing the tiny landing, the girls heard a voice calling to them from that empty room.

Then, as they watched in horror, long strips of wallpaper were torn off the wall in front of them by ghostly hands. "We just fled down the stairs and out of the front door. We were so scared that my friend was in hysterics. It was a horrible, horrible place. Even today I cannot pass it without feeling my flesh start to creep," shuddered Maureen. 🐦

Chapter Nine
SOME HAUNTED HOSPITALS

Hospital hauntings are frequent. There can be few institutions in which some sort of ghost — often a Grey Lady — has not been seen or heard wandering the wards and corridors in the early hours. Island hospitals at Ryde, Newport and East Cowes are no exception. Nurses and staff here seem to see more than their fair share of ghosts, possibly because they work in such close proximity to illness, suffering...and sometimes death. Could this make them particularly sensitive to the supernatural? Two nurses whose stories are told below have actually encountered ghosts in several wards at different hospitals. Here are a few tales to set the pulse racing.

GHOST IN TORMENT

An unhappy girl still weeps for her lost love at Fairlee Hospital, Newport, although both have been dead for many years. Her ghost is full of such sorrow that people working in the old staff quarters approached a priest to have her put to rest.

Mark Earp, who worked in most of the Island hospitals as a community porter, was greatly affected by the atmosphere in the old staff house at Fairlee — known familiarly as the "creepy coop". The ghost is said to be that of a lonely nurse who fell in love with one of the resident doctors. The affair went tragically wrong, and it is whispered that her body was found in a pool of blood at the foot of the stairs. No-one can remember after so many years, how or why she fell; the matter was hushed up. But the unhappy girl's ghost still walks...

Staff there have felt a rush of icy cold air passing them on the stairs and Mark has experienced her melancholy presence on three occasions. The first time he was on the top floor in what had once been the the dead girl's bedroom. "It was like walking into a fridge, the cold hit me like a solid wall and there was an awful atmosphere of hurt and of someone in pain."

The old staff quarters at Fairlee Hospital, Newport, once the scene of a tragedy

One night, Mark was photocopying in the room below when he felt something brush past him giving a low moan... something as cold as the grave. "I was scared out of my wits — there was no-one else upstairs. My hair was standing on end. It was as if something had pushed me out of the way."

His third encounter with the ghostly nurse came as he was walking upstairs. Something unseen but very cold rushed past him. "She was obviously in great distress and giving off an aura of terrible sadness. I talked to several other members of staff about it and we decided something had to be done. People often heard her weeping and moaning; the sorrow she radiated seemed to intensify at certain times of the year.

"I spoke to the priest, who agreed the place seemed to be haunted by a young woman who was very troubled and that her poor soul should be laid to rest. However, this was never done," said Mark. "So she wanders the building still, in her grief and torment."

The now-empty Niton Ward where a ghost tried to feed patients with porridge

SHE TRIES TO FEED US PORRIDGE...

In the old Fairlee Isolation Hospital itself, a ghostly figure in a long grey dress trimmed with a little white lace collar, was often seen by nursing staff on night duty at Niton Ward, where she sometimes startled elderly patients by trying to feed them porridge.

Known affectionately as the Grey Lady, she was frequently seen at night disappearing into the bathroom, where she would seat herself on an invisible low chair or stool and then vanish.

Mrs Anne Broad of Cowes, a local town councillor and union shop steward who worked on Niton Ward as an auxiliary nurse for several years, still vividly remembers seeing the hospital ghost gliding past her into the bathroom one night.

The ward, which was closed in the mid-1980s, was situated behind the Island's hospice, Earl Mountbatten House, and was originally used to isolate patients with infectious diseases. When Anne worked there, Niton and neighbouring West Wight Ward housed elderly patients needing respite care or long term attention.

Thirteen years of nursing had prepared Anne for some strange sights, but nothing to compare with that of the Grey Lady in her early Victorian costume. "She looked completely solid and although we often heard her footsteps on the ward, when she walked by me that night there was no sound at all. It was spooky but I wasn't really frightened. She seemed to belong there and never harmed anyone."

The Grey Lady always followed the same route between the ward and bathroom. Other nurses would see her sitting in the corner of the room intent on her sewing. There was also a presence in the ward kitchen, where nurses often had the uncomfortable sensation that they were being watched.

Patients, too, met the ward ghost. Sometimes the old ladies would complain that they had been disturbed during the night by a lady in grey who was trying to feed them porridge!

In neighbouring West Wight Ward, a lonely figure was seen at the dead of night sitting at the day room piano, long after all the patients were asleep. What haunting melody the ghost was playing, nobody knows.

THE GREY LADY OF CALTHORPE WARD

The Royal Isle of Wight County Hospital at Ryde also had its own Grey Lady who was frequently seen in the ground floor Calthorpe Ward. Over the years, staff heard and saw many supernatural comings and goings in the Victorian buildings, now no longer used by patients.

When she started her training at Ryde in 1964, Edwina Palmer at 34 years of age was one of the oldest nursing students there. Now a Cheshire Home resident, Edwina remains cheerful in spite of her twin handicaps of multiple sclerosis and rheumatoid arthritis.

The appearance of the ghostly Grey Lady was said to foretell a death on the ward. And one morning in the early light of dawn, Edwina saw her at the head of a patient's bed in Calthorpe Ward. "I was working in the children's ward

Calthorpe Ward at Ryde Hospital where a Grey Lady was seen and heard

opposite, when I saw a shadowy figure in grey with a short veiled head-dress, standing by a bed looking out of the window. I told the senior nurse who was so horrified she almost dropped the baby she was feeding," Edwina said. "I didn't go near Calthorpe for a few days because I was afraid I might hear that one of the patients had died," she added.

Footsteps would ring out in empty corridors at dead of night, and it was common for night staff to hear a man's heavy tread in a passageway between the ENT and gynaecological wards.

Another favourite place for phantom footsteps was between the private wing and the corridor to Calthorpe Ward. Nurses on night duty would often camp out in the tiny kitchen, dozing in comfort with the oven on low, while the rest of the hospital slept. "We always kept an ear open for the Sister," Edwina said. "She wore heavy leather shoes so if we heard her pounding down the corridor towards us, we would hastily straighten our uniforms and hide anything we had been eating or drinking.

"All too often however these footsteps would stop — just outside the door. We would be standing there to attention, but when she did not appear we looked out into the corridor and it would be completely empty."

THE GHOST'S GENTLE TOUCH

A matter of months before the last patient left the old Ryde hospital for good, Ruth Powell, a state enrolled nurse who lives at Shanklin, encountered the Grey Lady and even felt her gentle touch.

Over the years since Edwina had seen the ghost, the awful consequences said to follow a sighting had faded. No longer was she considered a harbinger of death. The Grey Lady of the 1990s was thought to be the shade of a nun who died at the hospital during the last war. Wearing a grey habit, she was seen sitting in an armchair in the day room. Sometimes she would glide around Calthorpe and Mary wards during the hours of darkness where agitated patients occasionally glimpsed her as she vanished through walls.

Ten years after she first started nursing at Ryde, Ruth finally met the Grey Lady for the first time at 2 o'clock one morning. She had gone into the women's day room near Calthorpe Ward for her break, snuggled down in an armchair under a blanket for a snooze, and...

"I woke suddenly to feel the blanket being moved. It was lifted up and tucked over my chest around my shoulders. Although it was dark, I was aware of someone in the room with me and I thought I must have overslept. I grabbed my hat and shot out of the room to the ward where the other girls were having a cup of tea.

"None of them had been in to wake me — I had been asleep for only half an hour and they were surprised to see me. It was the Grey Lady who had tried to cover me up. I believe she had been watching over me as I slept. Although she meant me no harm, I was too frightened ever to go into that day room again after dark."

The old Children's Ward at the Royal IW County Hospital at Ryde, where a ghostly nurse would inspect the sleeping children

GHOST ON HER ROUNDS

Joan Steel grew quite accustomed to the hospital ghosts when she worked the night shifts at Ryde. Now retired from nursing, Joan of Cross Street, Newport, remembers how the doors to the children's ward would suddenly swing open and a cold draught of air would 'swish' past the startled nurses keeping watch over the sleeping children.

Five minutes later those doors would open again as the phantom nurse finished her inspection of the ward and left — but this time the doors swung outwards, Joan recalled.

"There was a story that the ghost was a dedicated nurse who had committed suicide after a child in her care had died, and that she continued to walk the wards even after death to look after the sick babies and children," she said.

While working on Calthorpe Ward as an SEN in the late 1960s, Joan frequently heard the Grey Lady wandering the ward. "I never actually saw her but I would hear the swish of her skirts and her footsteps walking from bed to bed and then back down the corridor. They were definitely a woman's footsteps and most of the nurses heard them there at night," Joan said.

The hospital ghosts were an accepted fact of life there, for when she first joined the staff at Ryde hospital, one Sister told Joan, "You will probably hear all kinds of strange noises down here, but don't you worry, it is only the friendlies."

Joan never was worried by her experiences there. The ghosts moved around in the dead of night disturbing no-one. The patients rarely saw them and those staff who did, were not bothered by their presence. "They never hurt anyone and I believe they were just doing what they had always done — looking after the patients," Joan said.

HAND ON A BED-PAN

Nurse Ivy Griffith had a bizarre encounter with the ghost of one of Ryde hospital's old nurses one night. Ivy had gone upstairs to fetch a bed-pan for a patient from the sluice room, but as she took one off the shelf, a hand shot out and grabbed it back. That hand belonged to a nurse dressed in what looked like a late-Victorian nurse's uniform.

For a ghost she was surprisingly strong, and as Ivy yanked the bed-pan away from her again, the phantom nurse pulled it back. It developed into quite a tug-of-war. "If anyone had come into the sluice then, they would have had the fright of their lives to see a bed-pan floating through the air like that," laughed Ivy.

Once a refuge for aged and disabled seamen, Frank James Hospital at East Cowes has two seafaring ghosts

SAM THE SEAMAN'S GHOST

When she was working at Frank James Hospital, East Cowes, Ivy was most indignant when the Night Sister accused her of smoking in one of the corridors. "It's not me, it's Sam, our hospital ghost, he's been smoking again," she told Sister.

The old cottage hospital, now a Community Hospital, caring for geriatric patients, was originally opened in 1893 as a refuge for aged and disabled sailors. Sam, a whiskered old sea-dog, died there many years ago but his spirit did not apparently feel the need to weigh anchor and move on.

His ghost still limped around the hospital corridors at night and Ivy, with her strong psychic abilities, saw him clearly. "He is a short and rather fat little man with only one leg, and we would often hear him tapping his way round the hospital on his walking stick. He had a wooden leg, one of those that looked like half a broom handle, not a proper artificial one like you see today," Ivy recalled.

Sam wore an old black bosun's jersey and black trousers. He had a bushy beard and puffed away at a big carved meerschaum pipe. The ghost told Ivy he had contracted a tropical disease, and fearful of dying in a foreign land, insisted on returning to his home port. He was taken to the Frank James Memorial Home but neither nursing nor the East Cowes air could save him.

It was usually around 2am when Sam was heard stomping down the corridor. "He is a lovely old soul and would often give me a wink... and then walk right through me," Ivy said.

Sam is not the only old sailor who lingered with the living at Frank James. Ivy never discovered the identity of the hospital's other ghost, but he too was a man of the sea, a tall upright figure wearing a naval officer's uniform.

A more stand-offish spirit, he too smoked a pipe, but this one smelled atrocious. Nurses working nights would always know when he was on a tour of duty around the hospital wards, making sure all was 'shipshape and Bristol fashion'.

THE WORKHOUSE GHOST

Originally opened in 1774 to house up to 600 paupers, the Isle of Wight House of Industry — or the Workhouse as it was more commonly known — can still be seen at St Mary's Hospital, Newport. For until the Island's new multi-million pound high-tech steel-clad hospital was officially opened in 1991, old wards in the former workhouse were still being used by geriatric patients.

It was here, in the old Newport Ward, that staff would hear the sound of dragging footsteps crossing empty store-rooms overhead. When she transferred from Ryde Hospital, Joan Steel also experienced that curious phenomenon.

"The first night I worked there I heard a peculiar noise, as though one of the elderly patients was upstairs walking with a stick or zimmer frame. I immediately checked to see if anyone was out of bed, but they were all present and correct," said Joan.

Reluctant to leave her patients and go upstairs by herself, she rang the charge nurse, and while they were drinking coffee, he heard the footsteps too.

Part of St Mary's Hospital, Newport, was formerly the Island's workhouse

"This time we both went to investigate. There was no-one up there and nothing was out of place. After a few nights working on the ward I realised this was a regular occurrence which all the nurses heard. It would last for approximately two minutes and had apparently been going on for many years."

Whatever haunted nearby Wootton ward — also part of the former workhouse which is now closed — was not so harmless however, and nursing staff hated to be alone there at night.

"It was as though you were always being watched. It was a very uncomfortable place to work and there was an unspoken agreement among nurses that they were never left by themselves there," recalled Joan.

Late one night she took her break in the nearby day room but while she dozed, phantom fingers plucked at the chain she was wearing around her neck and twisted it so tightly that she woke in a panic, almost unable to breathe.

"It felt as though the chain had been wound around someone's finger. It was quite horrible. I never dared to sleep in there again," she admitted. ❦

The famous Victorian photographer, Julia Margaret Cameron

Chapter Ten
SMILE PLEASE — GHOSTS ON CAMERA

Most ghosts are extremely camera shy and they are rarely captured on film. In this chapter however, not only does the spirit of the famous pioneer photographer Julia Margaret Cameron linger, there is also a photograph in which the face of a young man has appeared... three months after his death. You will also meet a ghost which enjoyed travelling by car and another which haunts a library.

A RUSTLE OF SKIRTS

The unique images created by Julia Margaret Cameron, that formidable Victorian pioneer photographer, live on more than a century after her death... as does the lady's own spirit.

Mrs Joan Howard who has lived at the photographer's former home, Dimbola, since the late 1960s, still hears the rustle and swish of her long silk and taffeta gowns as she moves about and is often aware of her presence on the stairs.

Joan and her husband John once ran Dimbola as an hotel and guest house but now it is just their home. "We actually sold it once," said John. "But we knew immediately that we had made a mistake and we bought it back again six months later. There is a wonderful tranquil atmosphere here. It is like taking a step back in time."

During the years Mrs Cameron spent at the house she named Dimbola, overlooking Freshwater Bay, she took and developed almost 3,000 photographs there, turning her hen-house into a studio and the coalhouse into a darkroom.

A friend of the Poet Laureate Alfred Lord Tennyson, she persuaded celebrated visitors to his home at nearby Farringford House to sit for studio portraits — Ruskin, Darwin, Longfellow and Robert Browning among them.

It was during a short visit to Farringford in 1860 that Mrs Cameron on impulse agreed to buy a couple of houses from Jacob Long, an old sailor who dabbled in bricks and mortar when ashore. The houses were linked together,

Dimbola today, where Mrs Cameron took over 3,000 photographs and where her spirit still lingers

furnished and christened Dimbola after one of the Cameron estates. And it was here, in Ceylon in 1879, where Mrs Cameron died at the age of sixty-four.

Joan who used to do a lot of photography herself loves Dimbola and feels a strong affinity with Mrs Cameron's spirit. "When I go upstairs she is often there in front of me," said Joan. "And when we are sitting watching television I am aware of her in the corner and I sometimes hear her walking past me, her long skirts rustling as she moves about."

CAN A GHOST BE PHOTOGRAPHED?

Can a ghost be photographed? This one was certainly keen to appear in a family snapshot which was taken more than 60 years ago. It has been examined and authenticated by the Society for Psychical Research, according to Alan Jerome who has kept the tiny black and white print safe for all those years.

Hubert Jerome's photograph of his mother-in-law, showing the ghost of a near neighbour, peering out of the shrubbery

At his home overlooking the River Medina in Fairlee Road, Newport, Alan explained that the photograph had been taken by his father Hubert Jerome in 1928. It was simply intended as a snap of Alan's grandmother, Mrs Lucy Connard-Timmer, as she stood admiring the flowers in the back garden of the family home.

When the photograph was developed however, the face of a young man could clearly be seen to the right of Mrs Connard-Timmer and that face looked strangely familiar. Alan's father showed the print to Mrs Butchers, their next-door neighbour, who also recognised the face. "That's my Georgie," exclaimed a shocked Mrs Butchers.

She had every reason to be astonished, for young Georgie Butchers had died suddenly at home from appendicitis, three months earlier. The lad had been just twelve years old, and was a playmate of Alan's.

"He had very dark hair which he wore smoothed down with hair oil. I can still see that nipper as clear as day. I was two or three years younger than him

Detail of the ghost photograph — reproduced to show how distinct the image of the face is from that of the surrounding shrubbery

and it came as a real shock when we heard he had died in the night," Alan said.

Why young Georgie should appear in the photograph remains a complete mystery. His ghost had not been seen elsewhere, and it was not until the film was developed and printed that his image emerged.

"My grandmother was psychic and she had the gift of healing people with her hands. It may be that she was acting as an energy channel for spirits and that Georgie somehow managed to materialise on film. None of us ever saw his ghost in the garden that day, but the camera certainly did," Alan said.

THE JOY-RIDING GHOST

Not many ghosts travel by car — they generally seem content to get on with their haunting in a particular room or house. But one phantom who dwelt at a house in Weeks Road, Ryde, really enjoyed the occasional day out. Perhaps he just wanted a change of scene or some fresh air. Off he would go in the morning and home he came at night.

This unique ghost was already in residence at the three-storey house when a local family moved there some 20 years ago. Several previous owners had already left in quick succession and soon after Ursula, Stanley and their seven-year-old daughter, Amanda, moved in they discovered why.

Now married and a teacher in Ryde, Amanda remembers how terrified she was when the figure of a man appeared in her room one night and sat on the end of the bed. "It was icy cold, and I could actually feel the weight as the shape settled on my legs. I screamed and screamed, but as my mother rushed in to find out what the matter was, he vanished."

The family later discovered that a previous owner had hanged himself in that bedroom many years before. Young Amanda was the only member of the family to see the ghost, who would usually appear between 7pm and 10 pm at night.

"I could sense him in the room with me. It really was a horrible atmosphere and my room always felt so very cold. I tried taking the dog and cat in with me, but they were aware of the ghost too. The cat arched her back and spat. The dog barked and all his hair stood on end. Both ran away."

During the day, the ghost would sometimes go with Stanley, Amanda's father, to his workplace — Millway Engineering at Golden Hill Fort, Freshwater. "It was incredible. As my father got into the car we could actually see the door behind him open. The car would dip as if someone had stepped in, then the door would close, and off they would go. Whatever was in there with him was invisible, and although he could sense the presence, it never bothered my father."

At work, however, it was a different matter. The joy-riding ghost frightened one young lad at the factory so badly that he left, and never returned.

The family were much luckier with their next house in West Street at Ryde. This one had a far friendlier entity — even the dog liked him. The former owners had carried out a lot of alterations, which had disturbed the dormant ghost. He was quite mischievous and loved to play with the television and light controls, often switching them all on at midnight.

The family would hear footsteps crossing empty rooms overhead and the sound of muttered conversations. One day, Amanda's mother actually saw two shadowy, grey, transparent figures talking in a corner of the room. "Whatever was there didn't bother us at all. It could be naughty at times but there was nothing malevolent and we just accepted it," Amanda said.

THE SPECTRAL BRIDE

Meanwhile, back at that Freshwater factory which is now called Kenwood Ltd., a spectral bride in a long white gown and veil has been seen gliding down the aisles. No-one at the factory knows what she is doing there or who she is. Was she jilted on her wedding day? And more intriguingly, did she ever encounter the ghost who came by car?

The bride's wraith was seen at the factory by former air-stewardess Angie Steel, who lives in Freshwater with her husband Ray. "I was working on the production line one afternoon when I saw a figure dressed all in white wafting about. She was quite thin and was wearing a long white dress and bridal veil. As she materialised the temperature dropped dramatically. I became freezing cold and my hands felt icy to the touch," Angie said.

Ray doesn't believe in ghosts, but after working at a large old house in nearby Court Road at Freshwater, he had to admit something supernatural was going on there. He and two mates were decorating the house for a new owner, but one room in particular kept giving them trouble. It felt 'wrong'. Ray was convinced that he was being watched, and in that upstairs music room the wallpaper refused to stick to the walls. Every morning the men would come in and find it had peeled off again.

The light bulb in that room always moved during the night when the house was locked and empty. It would travel through a partition wall to be hanging from a different light socket in the morning. "I couldn't wait to finish that job and get away," said Ray. "I learned afterwards that the place had always had a bad name and that local people would not go near it after dark."

THE WRAITH OF COMBLEY WOOD

A number of Island ghosts haunt a particular stretch of road and a whole chapter in *More Ghosts of the Isle of Wight* told their stories. Here is yet another.

It was a cold clear night in December 1992 when Stuart Fleming collided with a woman standing in the road at Combley Wood, Havenstreet.

A shocked motorist collided with a ghost in this lonely lane at Havenstreet

"At 2.30 am I was on my way home to Ryde from St Mary's Hospital where I work, when my headlights picked up the figure of a woman in the middle of the road. As I turned the corner she was there. I slammed on the brakes but she was too close. I knew I was going to hit her. She saw me too. Her eyes were wide with fright.

"There was no impact. I slammed on the brakes so hard that they were actually shredded, but when I looked for the woman's body there was nothing there. Instead she was standing in exactly the same stance looking towards me, but she was a few feet further down the lane.

"I got out of the car to see if she was hurt. As I turned briefly to shut the door she vanished. I went up and down the lane searching for her. I even went back the next day in daylight. I could still see my skid marks, but I never found any trace of her."

Stuart who takes a scientific interest in ghosts and the paranormal, observed that the woman was young, probably in her twenties and very tall. Although the figure was grey, it appeared to be solid and he could clearly see ribbon tied at her throat as though she was wearing a bonnet or cap.

"Although she appeared to be terrified, she did not seem aware of me or my car. To her we did not exist and I believe we were both in completely different dimensions."

GHOST BOYS OF NORTHWOOD PARK

The sound of children at play is a common occurrence at Northwood Park, Cowes. Their excited screams, shouts and laughter are often heard there, especially at dusk — for these youngsters have no homes or warm beds to go to — they are ghosts.

Several local people have encountered the noisy and boisterous little spirits. Some actually see and hear them, others just hear them or feel their touch. Jean and Brian Lewis who live in nearby Baring Road had a strange encounter with the ghost children one March evening in 1993, as they walked home with their two dogs across the old park.

"Our daughter Kimiko had gone away for a few days and we took our Alsatian, Sam, with us when we went to pick up her dog, Chadwick. As I entered the park, I noticed a misty grey shape moving in the bushes. Sam's hackles rose and all his hair stood on end. I thought it must be a peeping tom or something," said Jean.

As Brian had gone ahead, she hurried to catch him up. "Suddenly I heard the sound of children at play. It was so loud it was deafening. Incredibly there were only two of them, but they were screaming, shouting, and laughing at the tops of their voices.

"They were playing on a huge old tree, swinging up and down on the branches. The lads must have been about eight or nine years old and they were both wearing some kind of school uniform; short trousers, little blazers and school caps. They looked about sixty years out of date and very old-fashioned. There was something so strange about them, but they looked solid and real."

Dusk was creeping towards full darkness by this time and Jean was worried about the boys being out so late. "I was rather frightened by the thing I had just seen in the hedge and I went up to the children to tell them to run along home. 'Go home. Only your mothers will cry', I told them. Why I said this I have no idea — the words just came out."

Here in Northwood Park at Cowes, ghost children still play

The boys however were completely oblivious to Jean's presence. "They didn't seem to be aware of me at all. They were swinging up and down on the tree so violently that the great branches were almost touching the ground; they were creaking and cracking. I could see the face of one of the boys. It looked grey and somehow too old for his body."

As Brian and Jean stood in the park that cold, still evening, the church clock struck seven. "I sensed something was very wrong. The children were taking no notice of Jean at all. I told her to come away at once," said Brian.

Still worried for the children's safety, Jean wanted to ring the police when she got home. "We had quite an argument about it," she admitted. "As it turned out I am glad we didn't because when our daughter came round to collect Chadwick, I told her what had happened."

"Are you sure they were real, Mum?" Kimiko asked, and then told Jean that she too had heard the children there several times but had never seen them. She had sensed their presence around her, and Chadwick had sat down and refused to move, giving every appearance of being stroked and petted by invisible hands.

Northwood House, once the Ward family estate, was a Red Cross hospital during the 1914-18 war

Customers at Hairtalk, Kimiko's hairdressing salon in Cowes, also spoke of ghostly encounters in Northwood Park, and one local medium confirmed Jean's description of the ghost-boys. They often came up to her when she was sitting in the park, she said. Other customers were reluctant to walk there after dark. They, too, had encountered the boys.

Jean and Brian have returned to that same tree several times since March in the hope of seeing them again, without success. They have also discovered that there was once a private school nearby, where in 1918, several children died during a virulent epidemic of Spanish Influenza which killed hundreds of thousands of people worldwide.

"The park is always floodlit after dark, but that night there were no lights at all. This has set me wondering whether we were in some sort of timeslip and for a brief moment had stepped back into the past," mused Brian.

Northwood House was built in 1837 on the site of a former residence, called Belle Vue, by George Ward and was later given to the local council for the people of Cowes. Believed to have been designed by John Nash, it was the largest house in the town. Between 1902 and 1906, it was occupied by a community of Benedictine nuns, who later moved to Appley, and Jean now wonders if it was the ghost of one of one of these sisters that she saw flitting through the bushes that night. She added, "Northwood Park is lovely in daylight... but at night it is a very different and disconcerting place."

SHHHHHH...

A very literate ghost makes little effort to stay silent among the books at Ventnor Library. Over many years, staff at the town's library, which now houses the Island's valuable music collection of 40,000 manuscripts, books and scores, have grown accustomed to the sound of footsteps coming from a locked room upstairs.

Ian Snow, who spent almost forty years as librarian in charge of Ventnor, often heard those phantom feet moving about the locked 'stack' room overhead. Shortly after his appointment there in 1953, Ian was sitting eating his lunch when he heard the footsteps above his head.

"I thought someone must be locked in the 'stack' but when I went to get the key, I found the door fastened and the room empty. Since then I have heard the footsteps countless times — and so have staff working there with me," said Ian.

"It is a benign presence which certainly doesn't do any harm. However it is impossible to tell whether it is a man's or lady's footsteps. We would hear them at any time of day, but most often at lunchtime. Two workmen painting the skylights noticed the sound of footsteps coming from the empty library and told me, 'You've got a ghost here.' They were a bit taken aback when I said we often heard it," Ian recalled.

Once when the roof was being renewed, Ian went up to check after the workmen had left that the doors and windows were secure. Suddenly the sound of angry stamping feet was heard coming from the roof valley. Had the ghost been disturbed by the work and gone up to find out what was going on, wondered Ian.

Senior Assistant, Valerie Bridgeman, who took over when Ian retired, also hears the footsteps and sometimes the sound of a box being dragged across the floor. Staff working in the music 'stack' have felt an invisible presence watching them, especially in the late afternoon.

Meanwhile downstairs, Valerie has been having a problem with the library borrowers' cards. "We keep finding them in the wrong place. When people return books, the tickets are under the wrong date. It is as if someone has moved the cards forward several days to give the borrowers extra time."

It is thought that the library originally started life as a theatre in the 1840s. It later became the Literary and Scientific Institution Reading Room and Library, and in 1866, the Literary Institution School was opened. Here at the school about 160 tradesmen's children were educated, with the boys being

Phantom footsteps can be heard in the music stack at Ventnor Library

taught at the library and the girls being housed in West Street. In 1940 the building was taken over by the council and is now under the control of the county cultural services department.

So who do those phantom footsteps belong to? Next time you visit Ventnor Library, listen carefully as you browse among the books. You might just hear a noisy ghost moving about that locked music room. ❦

Chapter Eleven
THERE'S NO PLACE LIKE HOME

Some ghosts seem reluctant to move on. Years after death they continue to make themselves quite at home in their former residences — which can be rather disconcerting for the current owners.

GHOST IN A DRESSING GOWN

One morning several years ago, Mrs Betty Bryan lay in bed telling herself it was time to get up. It was light, and she began to run through the list of her day's chores in her mind. Glancing at the mirror, she was startled to see the reflection of an elderly lady wearing a new pink dressing gown looking back at her.

"I recognised her immediately," said Betty. "It was old Mrs Hodder who used to live in the bungalow before I moved in. We had met several times. She appeared to be quite real and solid, and was trying this dressing gown on and looking at herself in the mirror."

Mrs Hodder had died the year before, and Betty moved into her council bungalow in peaceful Sunset Close, Freshwater. Intrigued by what she had seen, Betty told the old lady's grand-daughter about the apparition. She recalled that her gran had bought a new pink dressing gown through a catalogue club just three days before she died. However the old lady had never had the chance to try it on while she was alive.

Instead, Mrs Hodder appeared in her new dressing gown just a year after her death. "She looked very nice in it. It suited her very well," said Betty. "Perhaps some ghosts do care about what they are wearing. Mrs Hodder certainly did and that dressing gown fitted a treat."

Betty saw the old lady again in 1988. However this time she appeared upset and agitated. "The ghost was pacing up and down and did not seem aware of me at all," she said. Betty later discovered that on the same night, Mrs Hodder's granddaughter had been rushed into hospital where she had died shortly afterwards.

A ghost in a pink dressing gown was seen at this Freshwater bungalow

Since then the old lady's ghost has not returned, but just once a small dog has run across the sitting room floor and disappeared into thin air...a little ghost dog searching for his dead mistress perhaps?

THE NEIGHBOURLY GHOST

When Margaret and her husband Ron moved into their new home at Lushington, Wootton, they never expected to meet Mrs Smith, the former owner...for she had died there several months earlier. But as Margaret busied herself unpacking their belongings and making the house into a proper home for them and their young son Jeff, she started to feel she was being watched.

"As I went up the stairs I always felt uncomfortable, and by the time I reached the landing I would run across it. There was an unpleasant feeling there at the top of the stairs which I couldn't explain," Margaret said.

This went on for several weeks until one day, when she was alone in the house, Margaret felt a strong urge to look behind her as she went downstairs. "There was an elderly lady standing there behind me. She had long hair plaited across her head and she was dressed rather quaintly in a drab-coloured ankle length skirt. She seemed to be aware of me, and I suddenly had a funny feeling that the house was right for us, that we were being accepted there."

Realising she had just seen a ghost, Margaret described the "funny old lady" to her neighbour, who told her that it was old Mrs Smith who had died in the first bedroom off the landing. The Smiths had moved in when the house was built in 1938, and had lived there all their married lives until Mr Smith died and his widow followed soon after.

"I have never seen her since that day, almost 25 years ago, and after that I was never afraid to cross the landing again," said Margaret. "Perhaps she just appeared that day to show me she was there and that she approved of us moving into her old home. I like to think so anyway for she looked a very kind and friendly ghost and we think of her with affection. Even now occasionally a door will open by itself for no reason and whoever is in the room will call out 'Hello Mrs Smith'."

AN EYE FOR THE LADIES

A very lofty elderly ghost with an eye for the ladies appeared in his former Northwood home several years after his death. The grey-suited figure was so tall that Mrs Ellen Weeks never saw his head.

Mrs Weeks, her husband Eric and son John, moved to the old bungalow in Pallance Road in 1972, to look after her ailing father-in-law, Mr George Weeks.

As she was coming out of her bedroom one day, Ellen was alarmed to see a very tall man wearing a grey suit standing in the hall. When she described the figure to neighbours and her father-in-law, they recognised it as the old gentleman who lived at the bungalow until the Weeks family bought it in the 1950s.

"After that, he would appear at intervals although I only ever saw him standing in doorways. He seemed to stay around the hall. Often we would smell his pipe tobacco. It always smelled like it had just been lit, very strong and pungent."

A visiting friend actually felt his ghostly hands on her shoulders as she was sitting in the lounge one evening. "I am told that the old chap was quite a one for the ladies — even after death it seems," said Ellen with a smile.

The old bungalow has recently been demolished, and a new one built on the site. So far, the ghost has not put in an appearance. The family are waiting...

SPIRIT AT THE CASTLE

A group of children blackberry picking at Carisbrooke Castle, years ago, ran home crying to their mothers because they had seen a ghost in The Shrubbery.

Young Ella Morris, who lived at Upper Shide Mill, Newport, came in for a good scolding from her mother because she had been strictly forbidden to

Ghosts still walk near Carisbrooke Castle

A Victorian lady appeared one night near the castle moat

play near the old castle. Then she sobbed out her story of how they had seen the phantom of a huge man in a long white gown glide silently out of the bushes past them.

Strangely, although the castle itself is said not to be haunted, over the years apparitions have been seen outside the massive stone walls and ramparts and near the moat. Several years ago, Alan Burgess of Freshwater, who was serving in the Royal Navy at the time, went out for a stroll around the castle with his girlfriend one evening.

Coming towards them through the gathering darkness he noticed a lady walking her little dog. As she drew nearer, Alan could see she was dressed all in grey in what appeared to be a Victorian costume. She was gliding across the grass and away from the castle's main entrance. Alan stood rooted to the spot, incredulous and open-mouthed. His girlfriend wanted to know what the matter was. "She thought I was making it up just to frighten her. She simply couldn't see the Grey Lady at all," said Alan.

GRAVEYARD GHOUL

Across the other side of the village, two young boys taking a forbidden short cut through St Mary's churchyard at Carisbrooke one dark night, had the fright of their lives when they saw an elderly woman gliding towards them across the grassy mounds of the graves. She was a short, dumpy old lady dressed all in black, and was wearing a shapeless black straw bonnet which hid her face.

The eleventh-century Church of St Mary at Carisbrooke, where an elderly apparition terrified two young boys

Dick Hall of St Mary's Road at Cowes, who is now retired, still recalls that long-ago night during the last war with startling clarity... and a shiver. As the boys watched open-mouthed, the ghost, for that is what she was, knelt down behind a grey and weathered tombstone. Two shapes rose from the grave and moved towards them. "I was absolutely petrified. We didn't wait around to see what would happen next. We took to our heels and ran," he said.

OLD MR GREY

Many years later Dick had another brush with the supernatural, this time at his new home in St Mary's Road, Cowes, when he met the previous owner's ghost standing at the bottom of the garden one moonlight night.

The old house still had an outside WC and Dick was making his way there when he saw the figure of a man framed in an aura of blue-white light. The apparition had grey hair, a white moustache and was wearing spectacles.

"He was a really nice-looking fellow and was wearing a grey jacket. I did not feel frightened at all. He smiled at me and then just disappeared. I knew then that I had just met a ghost."

Dick described the spirit to neighbours who told him he had encountered old Mr Grey, a tailor, who had died in the house. Neither Dick nor his wife Pat has ever seen Mr Grey since. "It was his smile that I liked. He seemed to be welcoming us to his old home," said Dick with a smile of his own.

Mr Grey's ghost appeared in the back garden of this Cowes house

THE WHISPERER

A hoarse and low whisper which breathed "David..." in the middle of the night had such an awful effect on young milkman David Colson that, years later, he is still loath to be alone indoors in the dark.

Now living at Shorwell with children of his own, David still shudders when he remembers that throaty voice calling to him out of the darkness. At the time, he was living with his grandparents, Jack and Lilian Wright, in their 300-year-old cottage in Carisbrooke Road, Newport. A lad of seventeen, David had never given a thought to the cottage being haunted but soon changed his mind after he had heard that voice. "It was there in the room with me and it was a dark, dead sort of tone that made my hair stand on end," he said.

After hearing it on two different nights, David would not sleep without a light on until his marriage to Carol a couple of years later. The young newlyweds lived in a flat on the first floor of the cottage where they were continually being disturbed by the sound of footsteps coming up the stairs towards them. "We would wait for them to reach the top and then fling open the door but there was never anybody there," David said. "We would both hear a slow heavy tread coming up to the door. It really was frightening."

At Christmas time, cards hanging on strings around the room started to swing violently and unaccountably. One day after Carol left for work at a local restaurant, David tried to leave the flat too. But to his horror he found the only door to the stairs was locked and bolted — from the inside — which was impossible because the original 300-year-old lock did not work. With growing dread he realised that whatever had locked the door was in there with him.

"I was very scared. Somehow I managed to hammer that lock open, then I rushed downstairs to my grandparents and spent the rest of the evening with them."

Soon after this, David and Carol moved to nearby Field Place and their flat was converted back into bedrooms. But whatever walked there continued to do so, and even appeared to David's gran one evening. She saw a dark figure standing in her bedroom doorway and thinking it was her husband going to bed, she called out, "Goodnight, love."

Then it dawned upon her that this was no human form. It was a ghostly stranger in a black cloak, and as she watched open-mouthed he simply faded away. "I think she really believed what I had told her about the cottage being haunted after that." said David.

PHANTOMS IN THE MALL

In nearby Carisbrooke Road or The Mall, as it is also known, an old man's heavy footsteps are heard at the same time every morning, trudging down a garden path. No-one at the three-storey terraced house can enjoy a lie-in. The sound of those work boots plodding towards the back door is enough to wake the dead!

Just across the road, two of the fine old Georgian terraced houses share the shade of a man dressed all in black who has been seen passing through the party wall.

Cottages at Carisbrooke Mall, Newport

At the home of Glenda and Peter Knight, the scruffy-looking ghost wearing a long dark coat, has been seen walking into the wall of their spare ground floor bedroom. A few feet away startled staff in the offices of chartered architect Graham Biggs would see him emerge from the party wall.

THE GHOSTLY GROCER

A century ago William Randall Jolliffe was the proprietor of a well-known grocery shop in Ryde High Street, selling provisions to the local gentry and townsfolk. Eggs, flour, butter, cheese, bacon, preserves and other comestibles were all stocked there.

In his brown leather apron with his shirt sleeves rolled up, Mr Jolliffe supervised the shop and gave favoured customers his personal attention. When he died, the business passed to his son, who continued to run it as H. G. Jolliffe & Son, Grocers, until his retirement some years ago.

After a spell as a wool shop, the premises on the corner of the High Street and Green Street, were taken over by Jane and Steve Bird who opened a new store in the mid-1980s selling beds.

"All was quiet there at first. It wasn't until we started knocking walls down that the ghost put in an appearance. It was as if he came to see what we were doing to his old shop," explained Jane.

He was a short, stocky ghost with a round face and quite a kindly smile. Once the bed shop was open, he would appear quite regularly to keep an eye on things. "I think he was aware of me and would stand at the back of the shop with his arms folded, watching me as I served customers, as if to say, 'Alright then let's see how well you can do it' " said Jane.

"I actually used to talk to him and have little one-sided conversations, especially when the shop was empty and I was feeling bored. I quite encouraged him and I was never frightened of his presence. He was quite a kindly old gentleman."

Sometimes Jane and Steve would see the ghost in his Sunday best clothes, complete with outdoor coat and hat, but most of the time he was dressed for work in his leather apron. His appearance was often accompanied by smells of lavender water and a pungent odour of old tobacco, and when the shop was shut for the night, the Birds would often hear him playing with the till.

"He was absolutely fascinated by it and would keep ringing the bell without opening the drawer. It was a modern till and we got quite used to hearing it going at night. The first time it happened, Steve rushed into the shop, thinking someone had broken in to steal our takings," Jane laughed.

The couple would sometimes hear noises coming from empty rooms in the three-storey building and mentioned some of the ghostly happenings to their elderly landlord. "Mr Jolliffe just laughed and told us he knew all about it, but unfortunately he died before we could get the story out of him," said Jane. "However we did discover that the shop and the one next door had been built more than a century ago by Mr Jolliffe's father and that it had been the family home for many years.

Perhaps the Jolliffe family once owned a black cat. For its ghost has been seen on several occasions and Jane has even tried to stroke it thinking it was a stray which had wandered in.

A ghostly grocer haunted this shop on the corner of Ryde High Street and Green Street

"I had got up in the night and was on my way to the bathroom when I saw a black cat lying on the stairs. As I walked towards it, the animal stood up and stretched. I bent down to stroke it. The cat felt furry but not solid... and simply disappeared as I watched."

When Jane told her husband of this strange experience, he admitted he had seen the cat too a few days earlier, lying in the same spot on the stairs. "I don't like cats and when I saw this one I called for Buster, our dog, to come and chase it out. As I moved towards it, the cat stood up, stretched, and slowly vanished, rather as the Cheshire cat did in Alice in Wonderland, except this one didn't leave its grin behind," said Steve.

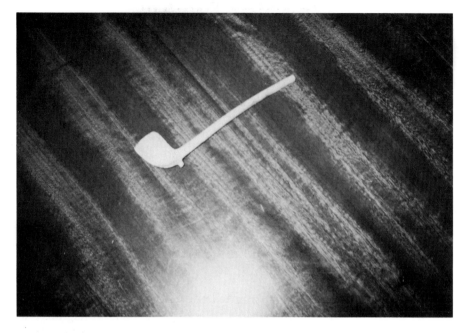

One of the old clay churchwarden's pipes, found during alterations to the shop

The phantom cat also made its presence known to local carpenter Alan Wood, when he was carrying out alterations for the shop's next owners, Mick and Maggie Jones. The startled workman complained of an unseen animal which kept rubbing against his legs.

Mick and Maggie who now run the shop as Babyneeds have never seen the ghostly grocer, but both occasionally smell his pungent tobacco smoke, and Mick found a collection of old churchwarden clay pipes hidden in a wall when the shop was being renovated.

Only when it rains does a ghost now appear in the shop. Maggie has twice seen the figure of a tall, elderly lady wearing a headscarf, standing near the front window. "I have not seen her face, but her clothes appear very old-fashioned, and she just stands there looking very wet indeed, then vanishes. The first time I saw her I looked to see if she had left a puddle on the carpet, but the floor was bone dry," Maggie said.

"I have no idea who she could be, but whenever it rains, I keep an eye open for that bedraggled-looking ghost taking shelter from the deluge." 🐾

Chapter Twelve
HAUNTS OF THE NOBILITY

The Isle of Wight has long been a favourite place of Royalty and over the centuries many old noble families have owned homes and estates here. They have left behind them a rich legacy of history and in two earlier books I have detailed hauntings at several of the Island's manor houses. Here we have a selection of ghosts — from the very highest in the land to their lowliest and most wretched servants.

THE GHOST WORE BLUE VELVET

Once it was a fashionable gentleman's residence set amid parkland overlooking the Solent. In its heyday, East Cowes Castle was a notable meeting place of society. Once described as "a piece of gingerbread Gothic", the castle with its crenellated grey walls, gargoyles and turrets was designed and built by the renowned architect John Nash in 1789.

Today nothing remains of this imposing edifice which was demolished in 1965 to make way for new houses. Few people can now recall what the old castle looked like or even where it stood. So when Leslie and Lily Angus moved into their brand new bungalow just off Hefford Road in 1986, they knew nothing about the history of the area... nor of the ghosts which still roam there.

A retired civil servant, Leslie had always laughed at the idea of ghosts until one June day in 1990 when one appeared in his living room. "The kitchen door was wide open and I noticed a small boy walking in from the garden. He stopped in the doorway and stood there watching us. Lily was with me; we both saw him. He was a little lad, about three years old and he was wearing an old-fashioned blue velvet suit. His golden hair was long and curly and he appeared to be from a very well-to-do family. He was a beautiful-looking child."

For a few seconds the little ghost-child stood looking at Lily and Leslie. "We thought at first it was a kiddie from a nearby house all dressed up for a party. I said, 'Hello, who are you?' He didn't answer and just vanished into thin air," said Leslie.

Photo courtesy of Bekens of Cowes

Once described as a piece of "gingerbread gothic" East Cowes Castle was a fashionable gentleman's residence

Exactly a year later, the young boy paid them a second visit. This time he was standing near the front door, still dressed in that blue velvet suit. Once again he vanished before their very eyes.

Since then Leslie and Lily have experienced some very strange happenings in their bungalow which stands on what was once the old driveway to the castle. They occasionally smell a heavy, cloying incense-like perfume which lingers in a corner of the living room where the little boy appeared. Other more appetising odours of newly baked bread and sizzling bacon also waft around the room.

Small objects such as keys frequently disappear, only to turn up hours later — exactly where they were left — when both Leslie and Lily have hunted high and low for them. The dining room will sometimes grow unnaturally cold; so cold that the air feels "as if a freezer door has been opened", said Lily.

Then at night come the noises. To the strains of a ghostly orchestra, she

Lesley and Lily Angus outside their East Cowes bungalow, where a ghost-child in blue velvet has been seen

and Leslie have heard the sounds of a party which seems to be taking place in their living room, usually between 2am and 3am. "We can make out a violin playing and guttural voices which seem to be speaking in German. The first time it happened I rushed in there only to find the room completely empty and in darkness," Leslie said.

"One night last year the noise was so loud we thought someone was trying to break in. We could hear glass smashing and the sound of doors being kicked. Whatever it was made a terrific noise which woke us up. Another night it sounded as though all the furniture was being thrown against the walls, but once again nothing had actually been touched."

Leslie suspects that a quantity of old bones which he found in the garden when excavating the footings for a shed, may have been connected with the haunting. "I don't know what the remains were, but they were brown with age and I put them in a couple of sacks and dumped them," he admitted.

"The noises started shortly after that. I reckon I have disturbed something which might have been better left buried."

*Above: Queen Mary was rarely seen
without her umbrella*

*Right: Holidaying at Cowes — was the
elegantly dressed ghost in Baring Road really **the Queen?***

AN UPRIGHT LADY

Meanwhile, across the River Medina, Nubia House off Baring Road and Egypt Hill, was one of the best known houses in Cowes until it was demolished in 1965. Home to the Baring family, the 35-room three-storey house was the rendezvous of high society, artists and politicians. Royalty were frequent visitors and Lillie Langtry, Edward VII, Edward VIII, George V, Princess Beatrice, Marconi and Gladstone were all guests at Nubia House.

All that remains of Nubia House — the ornate railings and gates where the Queen's ghost appeared

Queen Victoria Mary of Teck, Consort of George V, a close friend of Lady and Sir Godfrey Baring MP, would often take tea with the family at Nubia while her husband was yachting. Was it her upright and elegantly dressed ghost which was seen standing in the road outside the old gates to Nubia House? Mrs Jean Lewis believes it was.

Jean and her husband Brian live across the road from Nubia House in a property built on part of the former cottage garden. To the west of them, on land once known as The Soudan, was an asphalt tennis-court, the first hard court in Cowes. In the garden to the east, stood the coach-house, summer-house and Lord Baring's office.

It was shortly after they moved to Baring Road that Jean saw the regal-looking ghost. "I was looking out of my bedroom window at about 8am, one bright, crisp morning in March, when I noticed a very tall elegant lady standing in the road in very old fashioned attire. She was wearing a long black coat with the collar up. She had a long skirt, beautiful buttoned shoes and she was carrying a rolled umbrella. Her hair was swept up and she was wearing a hat.

"I thought she was one of the old Cowes gentry. She seemed solid and real. She stood there for a while, looking for someone, and then disappeared."

Jean later described the very erect and poised figure to Daphne, her neighbour. "I could have sworn she was dressed just like Queen Mary," she laughed. "Daphne then told me that the old Queen had been a frequent visitor to Nubia House and The Soudan, and that on one famous occasion in 1921 she had been sitting at the side of the tennis court drinking tea, when a tennis ball served by the young Sir Charles Baring had knocked the teacup out of the Queen's hand, spilling the contents all over her white dress.

Several other odd occurrences have happened at what was once The Soudan. The rear-view mirror in Jean's car was often adjusted at night by unseen hands. "Both the car and garage were locked, yet something moved that mirror to really crazy, extreme angles," she said. "I often experienced a cold uncomfortable feeling in that garage and felt as though I was being watched."

Echoes of the past are sometimes heard in the early hours of the morning. The murmur of ghostly voices and the sound of laughter can be perceived in the garden, coming from the site of the old summer house, where the Baring family and their royal guests would take tea during those summers so long ago.

Above: Swainston Manor, where a murdered maidservant's ghost is seen

Left below: The stone bridge at Swainston where a headless monk has been seen

THE MURDERED MAIDSERVANT

Swainston, one of the oldest and most important of all the Island's manor houses, stands in wooded grounds just off the Newport-Calbourne Road. It was here that a Freshwater woman encountered the ghost of a murdered maidservant fleeing from her killer.

Mrs Betty Bryan of Sunset Close, has seen the young girl's ghost on three separate occasions, each several years apart. Betty often walked past the manor and one day she noticed a girl, aged about eighteen, hurrying up the drive. She appeared very frightened and kept glancing behind her. Then, as suddenly as she had come, she disappeared, leaving a tangible feeling of terror in the air.

Betty encountered this pathetic shade twice more, and each time exactly the same sequence was re-enacted. Puzzled by what she had seen, she undertook some research and discovered in an old book about Swainston, a story which threw some light on the mystery.

This story told of Annie, a young maidservant, who was seduced by the rakish son of a lord of the manor. When she discovered she was 'with child', Annie confronted her lover one dark night, demanding money or marriage. There was an ugly scene and when she saw the murderous glint in his eyes, she tried to flee. But he was faster and stronger than the young maid. He gagged and bound her, pushing her down a steep incline. Her battered body was buried in a hastily-dug grave in the grounds. The murder went undiscovered and unpunished. The young lord never paid for his foul deed and still, centuries later, Annie's tormented spirit flees in vain from the hands of her killer.

There is another rather different version of the maid's story, in which it is said that she came to Swainston as a nanny but stole from her employers and her fellow-servants. Annie once purloined a silver brooch from the head housemaid, and her penitent spirit lingered at Swainston for hundreds of years until the little filigree brooch was finally found.

Now a five-crown country house hotel and restaurant, owned and run by the Woodward family who bought the manor in 1983, Swainston once belonged to the Barrington and Simeon families. It was extensively damaged by fire when hit by an incendiary bomb in 1941, but after being repaired, it was leased as a boarding school for junior pupils at the King James I Grammar School, Newport. Parts of the house date back to the 12th century and the manor, which boasts its own chapel, was once the summer palace of the Bishop of Winchester.

Perhaps this explains why the ghost of a headless monk is seen to walk over a stone bridge in the grounds, although no reason has ever been found for the appearances of the manor's Grey Lady who is said to glide across the landings upstairs. Manager Andrew Woodward has never yet seen either of his ghostly guests, nor have recent visitors to Swainston... the hotel has a warm, welcoming atmosphere which is probably enough to put any self-respecting ghost off its haunting.

THE RAVENSCOURT GHOSTS

Set high on a hill overlooking the Victorian town of Ventnor, Ravenscourt is the very epitome of a haunted house. Resembling an old Scottish hunting lodge, the striking grey turreted edifice looks certain to have a ghost or two.

A listed building, Ravenscourt is now the home of local councillor and former mayor of South Wight Borough Council, Alan Philpott and his wife

Ravenscourt — set high on a hill overlooking Ventnor

Jenny. It has been in their family for almost 40 years. Originally built in the 1830s and named Grove Mount, in 1892 the house passed into the ownership of William Mew Judd, innkeeper and owner of the Royal Marine Hotel. He changed the name to Heidleberg and added a three-storey tower at the northern end of the house. Successive owners have renamed it The Towers and Ravensnest.

The old house boasts at least three ghosts, one of whom is a fair-haired little girl in an old-fashioned party frock. Her shade has been seen several times by both Alan and his father as she flits past the kitchen window at the rear of the house.

Once when Alan was in the room by himself, he noticed a couple of children at the back gate. One of them, a small girl, walked up to the kitchen door. Thinking it was a child from one of the nearby holiday chalets, Alan went to see what she wanted. "By the time I could open the door she had vanished. I had definitely seen her and she looked solid and real. She was about ten years old and wearing a strange old-fashioned dress," recalled Alan.

The other ghosts were encountered in 1991 by an American friend who was staying at Ravenscourt, but who knew nothing of the house's chequered history. She came down for breakfast one morning, commenting on the two rather strange people she had just met on the landing.

"They were not modern people, they were old-fashioned from some time in the house's past," she told Alan and Jenny. "They were people from at least a hundred years ago and they were dressed like innkeepers."

THE JILTED BRIDE

More than a century after her lonely death, the sad shade of a reclusive spinster still haunts her former home. Jilted on her wedding day, Miss Margaret Catherine Dick withdrew from the world. Until her death 19 years later, she refused to leave the house at Bonchurch, afraid to face the world, the pity and the cruel gossip of neighbours.

Her pathetic story did however reach the ears of author Charles Dickens during one of his visits to friends in the village in November 1860. He was so fascinated by the tale, that a few weeks later, Miss Dick appeared in chapter seven of the serialised version of the novel *Great Expectations* on December 22, 1860, very thinly disguised as Miss Havisham.

The resemblances are clear. Miss Havisham, too, had been jilted on her wedding day. Dressed in her yellowing bridal gown and torn veil, with flowers in her white hair, she lived in a perpetual darkness lit only by candles, surrounded by decaying reminders of that tragic day; the wedding breakfast with its great bride-cake a playground for mice and black beetles — the hands of all the clocks in the house stopped at twenty minutes to nine.

The real Miss Dick whose remains lie in Ventnor Cemetery, lived alone at Madeira Hall in Trinity Road, a large, gracious home built some 250 years ago and said to have been a wedding present to the engaged couple. The Dick family were well-respected in the neighbourhood, at one time living at Upper Mount, now the Peacock Vane. It was on Captain Samuel Dick that the character of Mr Dick, one of the central figures in Dickens's *David Copperfield* was based.

Rarely emerging from the house, Miss Dick lived in an upstairs room which had a trap-door leading to the kitchen. Her meals were served through this hatchway by the daily woman who never saw her employer — her wages being left with the dirty plates.

When Miss Dick died at the age of 52, her mortal remains were laid to rest — but not so her spirit. That remained in the house where she lived out her lonely, loveless life. Miss Dick's ghost is still seen and heard today in the kitchens, bedrooms and corridors of what is now the Madeira Hall Hotel.

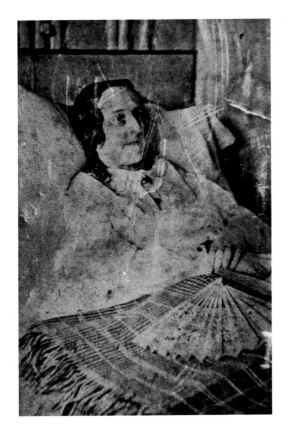

Catherine Dick — jilted on her wedding day

"We had no idea the hotel was haunted until we actually moved in," said Cindi Witheridge, who, with husband Peter, a petrochemical engineer, bought the listed building in 1989. They have spent a great deal of time and money renovating and upgrading it into a charming, comfortable country house hotel.

"The first week we were here we heard footsteps coming from empty rooms and a woman's voice exclaiming 'Oh dear, dear, dear, dear'. On another occasion she called out 'Helloeeeee' in a shrill voice", said Cindi.

Then Peter, a firm non-believer in ghosts, twice saw the misty grey figure of a rather dumpy middle-aged lady standing in the kitchen watching him as he used the meat slicer. On another occasion Cindi and Lesley, one of the hotel waitresses, were in the kitchen when a marmalade pot was snatched from Cindi's grasp by invisible hands. It flew under the table and came up the other side to land back on top of the table. "Lesley just screamed, and I was very shaken too. I didn't fancy marmalade for breakfast that day", admitted Cindi.

Despite this, the ghost of Miss Dick is never malevolent or frightening and the hotel has a welcoming and friendly atmosphere, attracting guests back year after year. "She is just very inquisitive, quite friendly and more than a little mischievous," smiled Cindi.

Guests sometimes meet a ghost at the Madeira Hall Hotel in Bonchurch

Miss Dick occasionally turns fridges off and sometimes in the mornings the family finds the kettle has been filled with water and set to boil by a ghostly hand, ready for their morning cup of tea. Zoe and Henry, the family's cavalier King Charles spaniels, refuse to have anything to do with Miss Dick, who they can sense in an upstairs room.

Peter and Cindi's teenage daughter Charlotte, however, is not at all bothered by her presence and has often seen the ghost and felt Miss Dick sitting on her bed.

The hotel's phantom likes to scrutinize and give her approval to the guests. Some visitors have seen the figure of a middle-aged woman wandering about the hotel. Her silver hair is worn in a tight bun and she is dressed in a blouse and long flowing skirt. One guest, a former hospital matron, was more than a little surprised when the figure approached her four-poster bed and tried to roll her and her husband out of bed.

A visiting vicar and his wife sensed the ghost's presence immediately, but told Cindi that she was quite a benign and friendly entity. Signatures in the visitors' book often comment on the ghost. One sensitive guest recently wrote that, in addition to the staff and other visitors, Madeira Hall was "full of friendly faces". Another said "Past expectations great, Great Expectations fulfilled". Another even signed in as a Ghostbuster!

In one particular bedroom there is often the scent of apples and a curious cold feeling. It was here, in this room where the trap-door can still be seen, that Miss Dick spent her nineteen lonely years. And it is also in this room that Cindi constantly has to rearrange the bedspread... to smooth away the indentation that appears at the centre of the bed where the ghost of Miss Dick has been taking a quiet nap.

THE END...

On that rather poignant and touching note I bring this third collection of Isle of Wight ghost stories to a close. When you finally turn off the lights tonight I trust you will sleep well. 🦇

Bibliography
AND FURTHER READING

Eldridge, R. J. — *Newport, Isle of Wight, in Bygone Days.*

Kokeritz, Helge — *The Place-names of the Isle of Wight.*

Page, William — *A History of Hampshire and the Isle of Wight.*

Heckstall-Smith, Anthony — *Sacred Cowes.*

Jones, Jack and Johanna — *The Isle of Wight, An Illustrated History.*

Searle, Adrian — *Isle of Wight at War 1939-1945.*

Garle, Hubert — *A Driving Tour of the Isle of Wight.*

Whittle, Tyler — *Victoria and Albert at Home.*

Winter, C. W. R. — *Manor Houses of the Isle of Wight* and
The Ancient Town of Yarmouth.

Green, Margaret — *Churches of the Isle of Wight.*

Tennant, Connie — *East Cowes, A Step into the Past*

Leal, H. J. T. — *Battle in the Skies over the Isle of Wight.*

Basford, Vicky — *Historic Parks and Gardens of the Isle of Wight.*

Hutchings, Richard T. — *Smugglers of the Isle of Wight.*

Fuller, Hester Thackeray — *Three Freshwater Friends.*

Dickens, Charles — *Great Expectations.*

Shepard, Bill — *Newport Isle of Wight Remembered.*

Jowitt, R. L. P. & M. — *Isle of Wight.*

Mew, Fred — *Back of the Wight.*

Moore, Pam — *The Industrial Heritage of Hampshire and the Isle of Wight.*

Insole, Allan & Parker, Alan — *Industrial Archaeology in the Isle of Wight.*

Chambers, Vincent — *Inns and Ale Bonchurch to Chale.*

Barron, William — *The Castles of Hampshire and the Isle of Wight.*

Isle of Wight County Press 1884-1934 — Jubilee Supplement.

Scott Daniel, David — *The Royal Hampshire Regiment.*

Cole, A. G. — *Yarmouth Isle of Wight.*

Index

GHOSTS OF THE ISLE OF WIGHT

ORDER YOUR SIGNED COPIES OF THE SPOOKY ISLE OF WIGHT GHOST BOOKS AUDIOBOOKS AND DVD

Gay Baldwin, 9 Pine Tree Close, Cowes, Isle of Wight, PO31 8DX, United Kingdom. Telephone: 01983 294651: **e-mail gb@hauntediw.demon.co.uk**

Original Ghosts of the Isle of Wight	£5.95	£..........
More Ghosts *(book two)*	£5.95	£.........
Ghosts of the Isle of Wight III *(book three)*	£7.95	£...........
Isle of Wight Ghosts *(book four)*	£7.95	£...........
Ghost Island *(book five)*	£7.95	£.........
Most Haunted Island *(book six)*	£8.95	£.........
Even More Ghosts *(book seven)*	£9.95	£.........
Knighton Gorges CD audiobook	£8.95	£.........
Ghost Island DVD	£12.95	£.........
Osborne House CD audiobook	£8.95	£.........

Postage is £1.20 each book. Postage for DVD is 80p. Postage is FREE for CD audiobooks (These prices are for postage to UK only, please contact me for prices if being sent overseas). Prices for DVD and CDs include VAT at 17.5%.

POSTAGE £ ....

TOTAL £............

Please make cheque/postal order payable to: **Gay Baldwin.**
Tell me if you would like it signed. You can order online at: **www.ghostisland.com**

Name..

Address..

....

....Post Code.............................

Telephone ....e-mail..